# The DALAI LAMAS
## of Tibet

'The Dalai Lama is like a ray of sunshine,
which is impossible for any one group of
people to obscure. The ray of Buddhist faith
will shine on everyone through him.'

—Manchu Emperor K'ang-si to the Seventh Dalai Lama

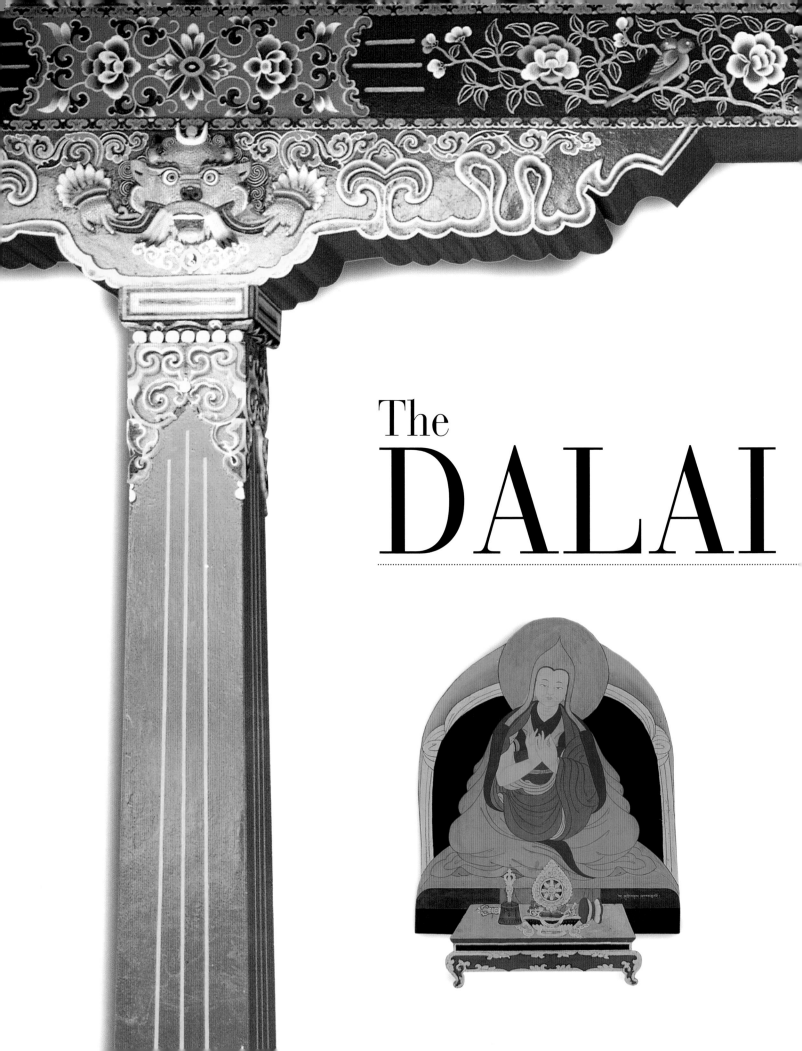

# The
# DALAI

# LAMAS
## *of Tibet*

HEIAN INTERNATIONAL INC.

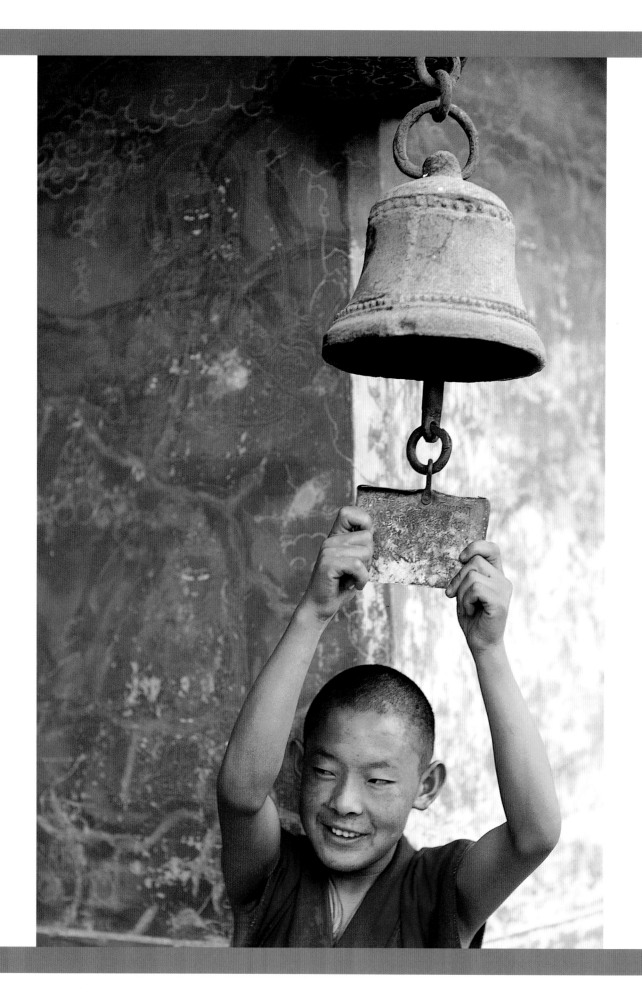

*To the children of Tibet . . .*
*in the hope that their future will be happier than our past.*

ISBN: 0-89346-918-1

**© Roli Books Pvt. Ltd. 2000**
**Lustre Press Pvt. Ltd.**

First American Edition 2000
00  01  02  03  04  05  10  9  8  7  6  5  4  3  2  1

HEIAN INTERNATIONAL, INC.
1815 West 205th Street, Suite #301
Torrance, CA 90501

Web Site: www.heian.com
E-mail: heianemail@heian.com

**Foreword:**
His Holiness the Dalai Lama

**Text:**
Thubten Samphel and Tendar

**Design:**
The Inkspot

Printed and bound in Singapore

# CONTENTS

Foreword by
His Holiness the Dalai Lama
11

*Chapter 1*
1959: The Story of the Year
15

*Chapter 2*
Origins of the Dalai Lamas
27

*Chapter 3*
God-Kings of a Modern World
51

*Chapter 4*
The Dalai Lamas: A Retrospective
71

*Chapter 5*
Tenzin Gyatso: The Fourteenth Dalai Lama
107

# FOREWORD

I am happy that Roli Books is coming out with a pictorial book on the origin and development of the Dalai Lama institution.

The institution of the Dalai Lama is about 400 years old, whereas Tibet as a homogenous culture existed for more than 2,000 years. According to some archaeologists, an organized culture flourished in pre-historic Tibet about 8,000 years ago. Besides this, we have our Bon culture, which existed in Tibet for about 4,000 years. If in some future time, the Tibetans decide that the institution of the Dalai Lama is of no benefit to Tibet, then the Dalai Lama institution will cease to exist. I have made this clear many times in the past and specifically in an official statement issued in 1969.

Like other institutions, the institution of the Dalai Lama has its great strength and also weakness. In times of crisis like the one we are now facing, the Dalai Lama becomes the rallying-point of the Tibetan spirit. At other times, the Tibetan people's dependence on one man and on one institution becomes a hindrance to the growth of Tibetan democracy. In view of this, starting from the early 1960s I introduced democracy into the exile Tibetan polity in the hope that in the absence of the Dalai Lama the Tibetan people's social and political cohesion is held together by deep-rooted democratic institutions. I also introduced democracy in the hope that this would encourage Tibetans to participate more vigorously in the political process and take more responsibility for the affairs of Tibet.

In 1992 I formally announced that in future when we return to a genuinely self-governing Tibet I will step down from my political leadership and will not hold any positions in the Tibetan Government. I have reiterated this many times since then. In fact, I am not even interested in any official position in the religious hierarchy. If I remain as a private individual, in times of crisis, the Tibetan people could turn to me as an honest, neutral arbiter of Tibetan affairs.

August 24, 1998

**1**

**2**

**3**

**7**

**8**

**9**

**13**

**14**

4

5

6

10

11

12

✿

*The Dalai Lamas of Tibet: A rare collection of mural paintings of the First to the Fourteenth spiritual heads as depicted on the walls of the main temple in Norbulingka in Dharamsala. Beginning in the fifteenth century with Gedun Drub, recognised posthumously as the First Dalai Lama, the institution of the Dalai Lama has gained in spiritual authority and temporal power with each successive leader. The Great Fifth, Ngawang Lobsang Gyatso, combined political wisdom with erudition; while the Great Thirteenth, Thubten Gyatso, steered the State through much political turmoil. The spritual influence wielded by the Fourteenth Dalai Lama, Tenzin Gyatso, is recognised the world over, as more and more people are drawn to the spirit of Buddhist philosophy.*
*PAGES 8-9: A monk in deep contemplation during one of the teachings by His Holiness the Dalai Lama.*
*PAGE 10: His Holiness the Fourteenth Dalai Lama in an introspective mood.*

✿

# 1959: The Story
# OF THE YEAR

On March 31, 1959, a sick, twenty-four-year-old Dalai Lama and his small and harried party left the last Tibetan outpost of Mangmang and slipped into Arunachal Pradesh in north-east India. He and his party had been travelling since March 17 when they had left Lhasa, the Tibetan capital, which was devastated by the turmoil· of Tibetan resistance and Chinese repression. Across the border a knot of soldiers of the Assam Rifles and some officials had gathered to receive Tibet's spiritual and political leader.

Little did the Indian officials know then that they were not just welcoming a few

*✿ FACING PAGE: From a Central Asian institution the Dalai Lama has transformed his lineage to a global spiritual powerhouse.*

Tibetan fugitives, albeit important refugees. They were, in fact, receiving a whole culture which had suddenly landed at India's doorstep.

'There was nothing dramatic about our crossing of the frontier,' notes the Dalai Lama in his autobiography, published three years after his historic escape to freedom. 'The country was equally wild on each side of it and uninhabited. I saw it in a daze of sickness and weariness and unhappiness deeper than I can express.'

In Tezpur the Dalai Lama was astonished and touched to find thousands of telegrams of good wishes and about two

*Traditional prayer and meditation rooms of high incarnate lamas.*

hundred journalists and photographers who had come to that remote corner of India to cover the story of the year.

With the Dalai Lama's escape to safety after the failed uprising against Chinese rule in Tibet, the history of Buddhist Tibet, as personified in the slender figure of the Dalai Lama, had come full circle.

More than 1,300 years ago, ardent Tibetans, who were sponsored by an equally enthusiastic state, had crossed to India in a constant stream to be able to take back to Tibet the wisdom and culture of Buddhist India. Within a period of three to four hundred years, the Tibetans had successfully completed the first conscious cultural transmission in history. By the eleventh century, Tibet had become a largely Buddhist country; according to traditional Buddhist chroniclers, the Tibetans, defying geography and gravitation, had succeeded, metaphorically, in persuading the obliging

waters of the Ganges to make the desert sands of Tibet bloom and, literally, in tempering their traditional martial instincts with the gentle teachings of the Buddha.

So, in 1959, most of the spiritual figures of Tibet, the living embodiment of the Tibetan Buddhist heritage, also sought refuge in India in the wake of the Dalai Lama. In doing so they brought back to India their Buddhist heritage which shaped their society and contributed to the

✿ *His Holiness the Fourteenth Dalai Lama in Dharamsala. He begins his day at four in the morning and ends it at ten at night.*

formation of their most important social and monastic institutions which enabled them to forge a unique civilisation. All this and more they brought back to the country of the origin of their faith in the hope that here they would be able to practise and promote their cultural heritage which had been brutally denied to them in their own country by an aggressive and inimical foreign force.

However, at the time, the Tibetans' trek across the world's highest mountains was

☼ *A mural painting in the Norbulingka palace in Lhasa; it depicts Tibet's spiritual and political hierarchy surrounding the Dalai Lama and foreign representatives to Lhasa.*

seen simply as another refugee exodus, the latest in the long line of assorted groups who had swept across India, either to invade and loot, or to escape political oppression and religious persecution. No one viewed it as an attempt by a people, undertaking an epic journey across the most treacherous mountains in the world, to save the soul of their nation, the heart of their culture, the breath of their gentle, mountain civilisation.

In India the Tibetan refugees not only found a welcoming sanctuary in which to rebuild their shattered lives and gather together the broken threads of their culture; they also stumbled onto the modern world and the rough and tumble of democracy. They had stepped out of their medieval world into the mid-twentieth century.

In exile, amidst India's teeming masses, the stunned refugees were able to build a viable and cohesive community supervised by a small bureaucracy, headed by the Dalai Lama. By example and constant exhortation he guided his greatly reduced parish towards the road to self-confidence and recovery. He gave them a sense of belonging and community in what the first refugees considered a strange land where the only thing familiar to them was the self-same earth and sky. The rest was so strange, so unfamiliar. By exiling themselves to India, the Tibetan refugees lost a country but in the process, they managed to create an empire.

The centre of the empire is a piece of hilly land, a mere few acres, bought with hard cash in the late 1960s, which houses the central Tibetan administration in Dharamsala in a breathtakingly beautiful part of north-west India. Like Shangri-la itself, the Tibetan exiles' imperial creation is more a state of mind than a continent-sized real estate. But Dharamsala, tucked away in a remote corner of Himachal Pradesh, forms the hub from where numerous spokes radiate to constitute the wheel of Tibet's burgeoning international constituency.

Except for the Jewish, no other people's diaspora has attracted such huge international attention. And no other people's struggle has entered the world's exile folklore with such fanfare, or is considered as the litmus test of whether the human spirit, after all, is able to survive the unrelenting buffeting of a totalitarian regime.

Behind the success story of the Tibetan refugees stands the remarkable figure of the Dalai Lama. He was only fifteen when, in 1950, he assumed responsibility for Tibet's political affairs after China invaded central Tibet. In 1959 when he was twenty-four, he lost his country and his inheritance.

The twentieth century is littered with disinherited, exiled leaders—the sometimes deserving victims of popular democratic upsurges—who have shrivelled into irrelevance because of their incapacity to

adapt to changed circumstances. But not the Fourteenth Dalai Lama of Tibet. He is growing increasingly relevant, not only to Tibet but to the whole world.

His youth, his humour, his open-mindedness and his Buddhist perspective on the vicissitudes of life has given him the strength and vision to restructure Tibet's traditional polity to facilitate the growth of Tibetan settlements, schools, enterprises, cultural institutions and monasteries. In doing so the Dalai Lama has not only made the Tibetan polity democratic and an active

*✿ Taktser, in Amdo, north-eastern Tibet, the birthplace of the present Dalai Lama.*
*FACING PAGE: Two nuns rest in the shade of their master and ultimate guide.*

and a growing part of the modern world but also transformed himself and the institution he inherited into one which has gained worldwide recognition.

Behind the personality of the Dalai Lama is the influence and power of the institution itself. The Tibetans believe that the Dalai Lama is the human manifestation of Chenresi or Avalokitesvara, the deity of Compassion, the protector of the Land of Snows. How the Tibetans view the Dalai Lama is best described by Rick Fields in his book *How the Swans Came to the Lake—A Narrative*

*History of Buddhism in America.* To Tibetans, the Dalai Lama was not only the political ruler of their country, he was the incarnation of Avalokitesvara. The basis of this rebirth was considered to be the Bodhisattva vow of Mahayana Buddhism—a deep motivation, strengthened through lifetimes of spiritual practice, to delay one's own entry into nirvana in order to liberate all sentient beings.

For centuries the outside world viewed the Dalai Lamas of Tibet as being as mysterious as the country they ruled. Both geography and Tibet's own isolationist policy effectively sealed off Tibet from the rest of the world; the little information on the country which did trickle out reinforced the world's view of Tibet as a Never-Never Land ruled by lamas who had the tendency to levitate and fly from one icy mountain peak to the other!

This view is patently false and does great disservice to the unique social contract the Tibetans had developed in the institution of the Dalai Lama, which, because of its spiritual weight in much of Central Asia, was inexorably drawn into the complex and turbulent politics involving Tibet, Mongolia, China, British India and Czarist Russia.

This view also does disservice to Tibetan cultural and spiritual influence which encompassed much of Asia. Traditional Tibet was the heart of a living civilisation

✧ *ABOVE AND FACING PAGE:* 'Be my guide, be my lamp To that goal Called Enlightenment.' *PAGES 24-25: The mix of politics and spirituality— a crowd with a Tibetan flag observes a major candlelight vigil for those in Tibet.*

and the Dalai Lama was its most potent political and spiritual symbol. There is no Asian equivalent to the Pope; but if there were to be one, it would be the institution of the Dalai Lama whose spiritual domain is not just confined to the political boundaries of Tibet, but spills over to Mongolia, western China, sizeable chunks of Russia and the entire Himalayan region.

# Origins of the
# DALAI LAMAS

To understand the origins of the institution of the Dalai Lama we need to go back to the history of Tibet before the emergence of the lineage. From the seventh to the tenth centuries Tibet was ruled by a line of emperors who united the Tibetan-speaking people and forged the country into an expansionist military state. Three of the most prominent emperors of Tibet's Yarlung dynasty patronised Buddhism, sent Tibetan students to India and invited Indian scholars to Tibet.

The last great emperor of Tibet, Tri Ralpachen, was murdered in 841 by his

*✿ FACING PAGE: New Year festivities in Lhasa at the base of the Potala Palace.*

older brother, Lang Dharma, who himself fell victim to an assassin in 846. After his death the empire disintegrated, and the whole of the Tibetan plateau became overlaid by numerous petty principalities and fiefdoms, each fighting the other and jostling for national dominance. Tibet remained divided for over three hundred years.

In 1207 the Tibetans learned that the hordes of Genghis Khan had destroyed the Tangut empire based along the borders of north-east Tibet. The Tibetans constituted a council of elders and sent a delegation to the Mongol camp to pay obeisance. Due to this, Tibet was spared a Mongol onslaught. Though it was integrated in the expanding Mongol empire, Tibet was never directly administered by the Mongol Khans.

The grandson of Genghis Khan, Godan Khan, appointed Sakya Pandita, a great Buddhist scholar and the abbot of Sakya monastery, as his spiritual preceptor and invested him with the temporal authority of Tibet. With the backing of Mongol military might, the Sakya lamas became the first in the line of priest-kings of Tibet and ruled Tibet for ninety-six years. The Sakya lamas were also the first to establish the concept of priest-patron relations or *cho-yon,* a determining factor in Central Asian politics. In return for spiritual guidance and the prestige and blessing of Tibet's lamas, the Mongols, and later the Manchus, guaranteed the protection of the Tibetan state from external invasion and internal strife.

Godan Khan was succeeded by one of the great Mongol monarchs, Kublai Khan. He became the supreme ruler of all the tribes of Mongolia and beyond, and in 1279, subdued China and established the Yuan dynasty—the first non-Chinese rulers of China. In Tibet, Sakya Pandita was succeeded by his nephew, Phagpa, who further strengthened relations with the

✿ Cham *or monastic dance in the shadow of the Himalayas is meant to dispel evil influence.*

powerful Kublai Khan and went on to become the imperial spiritual leader and the ruler of Tibet. When Phagpa was asked to become the Emperor's guru, the Tibetan lama agreed but on the condition that he sat on a higher seat when imparting teaching to the Mongol Khan. Kublai Khan at first refused but agreed when the Tibetan lama decreed that the Khan could sit on a higher seat during secular ceremonies. Phagpa also invented a new script for the Mongols which Kublai Khan used as the official means of communication throughout his vast domain.

In 1350 Changchub Gyaltsen of Phagmo Drupa, one of the governors of the Sakya lamas, revolted and terminated Sakya hegemony and Tibetan subservience to Mongol domination, establishing a secular rule in an attempt to give Tibet its former imperial glory. This was followed by the reign of the Ringpung kings who ruled Tibet from 1498 to 1565 and three Tsangpa kings who held the throne from 1566 to 1641. In 1642 the Great Fifth Dalai Lama, with the backing of his Mongol patrons, assumed temporal supremacy of Tibet and established the government of Gaden Phodrang.

By then Buddhism had become entrenched in Tibet. The political vacuum created by the lack of a stable central authority was increasingly filled by

✿ *Sand* mandala: *a lesson in the Buddhist view of the impermanence of life.* FACING PAGE: *Votive butter-lamp offerings to the enlightened ones.*

religious sects which aligned themselves to the political authority of the day to enhance the influence of their particular brand of beliefs.

Of the religious orders, four were most influential. The Nyingmapas, or the ancient ones, traced their lineage to the Indian tantric Padmasambhava who was invited by Trisong Detsen (742-798) to strengthen Buddhism in Tibet and who built Tibet's first monastery at Samye. The Kagyupas and their numerous sub-sects traced their lineage to Marpa (1012-96), the celebrated translator and teacher of Milarepa who is considered Tibet's greatest poet-saint. Marpa, in turn, traced his spiritual lineage to the Indian *siddhas* Naropa and Tilopa. A sub-sect of the Kagyu school, the Karma Kagyu introduced the practice of reincarnating lamas, which was later adopted by most schools of Tibetan Buddhism. The Sakya order was founded by Khonchog Gyalpo and his son Kunga Nyingpo (1092-1158). Unlike other schools, the Sakyapas based their power on hereditary succession and the Sakya lamas took consorts to produce sons to carry on the lineage. The Gelugpas and their predecessors, the Kadampas, traced their spiritual lineage to Atisha, the abbot of Vikramashila monastic university and one of the greatest teachers of Indian Buddhism, who visited Tibet in 1042 at the invitation of Yeshe O, the King of western Tibet, to restore the fortunes of Buddhism

in his kingdom. But these four major schools of Tibetan Buddhism were underpinned by a profusion of sub-sects as indicated by the Tibetan saying, 'Every lama his own doctrine, every valley its own dialect.'

All these sects established sprawling monasteries which became spiritual and cultural centres and which, in themselves, carried tremendous political clout. These orders were soon drawn into the struggle for political supremacy, primarily between the central Tibetan region of U with its base in Lhasa and Tsang with its base in Shigatse.

In this game, the Kadampas were waging a losing battle until Tsongkapa entered the scene. He was born in 1357 in Amdo, north-east Tibet, not far from the birthplace of the present Dalai Lama. His father was a local official. He received his monk's vows from Karmapa Rolpa Dorje, the hierarch of the Karma Kagyu. At the age of seventeen, he set out for central Tibet to receive instruction from the most famous teachers of all the schools of Tibetan Buddhism.

Despite the eclecticism of his spiritual education, when he turned forty, Tsongkapa enrolled into the monastery of Reting, sanctified by the Indian master Atisha who was considered by the Kadampa school of

*The glittering, gleaming roof of the Tsuglakhang in Lhasa, the Mecca of the Tibetan Buddhist world which houses one of the oldest images of the Buddha.*
*FACING PAGE: Two deer face the wheel of law on the rooftop of every Tibetan monastery, a constant reminder of the Buddha's Turning of the Wheel of Law (his first teachings) at the deer park in Sarnath, more than 2,500 years ago.*

Tibetan Buddhism as the mainspring of its lineage. At Reting, Tsongkapa wrote some of his most important works, including the *Lamrim,* the graduated path to enlightenment. In 1408 Tsongkapa, with the patronage of the Phagmo Drupa king Drakpa Gyaltsen, instituted the Monlam Chenmo or the Great Prayer Festival at Jokhang, the central cathedral in Lhasa. Tsongkapa, we are told, devised this festival as an annual rededication of the whole of Tibet to the Buddhist faith. In 1409 he founded Gaden monastery near Lhasa, which in time became the third largest monastery in Tibet with a reputed monk population of 3,300. He introduced strict monastic discipline and put high emphasis on the academic performance of the monks. At the time his order came to be called the New Kadampas and only later was it referred to as Gelugpa or the Virtuous Ones.

The increasing prestige of the order attracted a growing following, initially around Lhasa, and then from other regions. The growth of other monasteries around Lhasa, Drepung in 1416 and Sera in 1419, contributed greatly to the organisational might of the new order. Later, when the Great Fifth Dalai Lama assumed temporal authority of Tibet, the monastic universities of Gaden, Drepung and Sera, collectively referred to as the Three Great Seats, became his religious and political base.

*Every year thousands of devotees from all over India, Nepal, Bhutan and Tibet flock to receive teachings from His Holiness the Dalai Lama.*

The expansion of the Gelugpa order was facilitated by the fact that there was no organised opposition either from the other schools or from their political patrons. Tsongkapa died in 1419. His disciples, Gyaltsab Dharma Rinchen, Khedrub Je and Gedun Drub continued the work of their master. Gedun Drub founded the Tashilhunpo monastery in Shigatse, the second largest city in Tibet after Lhasa. The founding of this monastery in Tsang spread the Gelugpa influence beyond Lhasa and U. Gedun Drub remained the abbot of Tashilhunpo monastery till 1474 when he died at the age of eighty-four.

There is a sneaking suspicion among some scholars that Gedun Drub, posthumously recognised as the First Dalai Lama, might have engineered his own rebirth to add prestige to the Gelug order. Anyway, Gedun Gyatso, the Second Dalai Lama, born several years after Gedun Drub's death, was considered to be his reincarnation. Gedun Gyatso's reincarnation was discovered in Sonam Gyatso, who was born to a distinguished family with links to the royal household of Sakya and to the ousted Phagmo Drupa lineage.

The Gelug order was still untarnished by temporal power; its monastic simplicity and devotion contrasted sharply with the other orders' involvement in the constant civil and religious strife of the day.

But Sonam Gyatso took a step which, in retrospect, dramatically changed the fortunes of his order; he accepted an invitation to visit Altan Khan, the chief of the Tumet tribe of the Mongols. The two great figures met in 1578 near the shores of Lake Kokonor. The upshot of this meeting was that the Mongols increasingly became identified with the Gelug order in Tibet. Sonam Gyatso is reputed to be the one lama who finally converted the whole of Mongolia to Buddhism. The Tibetan lama was given the Mongol title of Dalai Lama by a grateful Altan Khan. *Dalai* is a Mongol word for ocean and *lama* is the Tibetan for teacher. Together the title *Dalai Lama* means *the ocean of wisdom*. Posthumously, Gedun Drub and Gedun Gyatso were regarded as Tibet's First and Second Dalai Lamas. This relationship was further cemented when Yonten Gyatso, the Fourth Dalai Lama, was discovered in the great-grandson of Altan Khan. This piece of divine providence ensured that the military might of Mongol tribes was conclusively laid at the service of the Dalai Lama and his order.

At this point began a troubled period of Tibetan history. The attempt by the nine successive lamas of the Phagmo Drupa lineage to reunite Tibet and give it a measure of peace, prosperity and stability failed. The Ringpung kings, who were

✧ *Ruins and newly restored parts of Ganden Monastery, Central Tibet.*

formerly the powerful vassals and allies of the Phagmo Drupa, ended the Phagmo Drupa hegemony with the aid of the Karmapas of the Kagyu order and elevated themselves as the shaky central authority. There was uninterrupted warfare which set the province of U against Tsang and the Gelug order against the Karma Kagyu, with their allies and fiefs changing loyalties according to the changing fortunes of war. Soon U or central Tibet was overrun by the

forces of the Ringpung kings and the centre of power shifted from Lhasa to lesser towns in the Tsang province.

By then the Gelug order had become sufficiently entrenched for the Karma Kagyu to see it as a potential threat. The Karma Kagyu's fortunes took a turn for the better when Tseten Dorje toppled the Ringpungs and set up his base in Shigatse, taking control of the neighbouring areas. Tseten Dorje and the two sons who

*○ RIGHT: His Holiness the Dalai Lama at the new Tsuglakhang in Dharamsala built in the 1970s; this currently serves as one of the important teaching sites in India.*

succeeded him came to be known as the Tsangpa kings and were staunch followers of the Karma Kagyu lamas. The Great Prayer Festival, instituted by Tsongkapa, was then banned and there were forcible conversions of small Gelug monasteries into Karma Kagyu. Tsang military camps were established outside Lhasa. One cut off the Drepung and Sera monasteries from Lhasa and the other blocked the city's main route to outflanking regions.

Gelug hopes were revived when Mongol troops camped outside Lhasa; but the Mongols were not prepared for battle and adopted a policy of wait and watch. This led people to say that the Mongols were 'too many for a gang of bandits and too few for an army'.

At this critical and defining moment in Tibetan history appeared one of Tibet's greatest figures, the Fifth Dalai Lama. He was born in 1617 in Tsang to a family which had traditional ties with the Sakya and Nyingma orders. Always politically astute, 'he realised the gravity of the situation and the dangers that faced the Gelugpas themselves,' wrote Giuseppe Tucci in *Tibet: Land of Snows.* 'But the decision he took was pregnant with consequences... He called in Gushri Khan to put an end to the long conflict and get the better of his powerful adversaries, Tsang and the Karmapas.'

Gushri Khan, the bearded twenty-eight-year-old chieftain of the Qoshot Mongols, first vanquished the Chogthu Mongols who were supporters of the Tsang king. He then entered eastern Tibet and subdued Donyo Dorje, the chief of the Beri tribe, another powerful ally of the Tsangpa king. After that he entered central Tibet and moved against the Tsangpa king himself who was captured. In 1642 the Fifth Dalai Lama travelled to Shigatse

where Gushri Khan conferred on him the supreme authority over Greater Tibet, a domain which stretched from Dartsedo, Tibet's traditional border with China in the east, to the borders of Ladakh in the west, and which roughly corresponded with the Tibet of the imperial age.

Back in Lhasa, the Fifth Dalai Lama declared his city as the capital of a united Tibet and the government of Gaden

Phodrang—the name of his palace in Drepung monastery, the new governing authority of Tibet. He instituted the office of *Desi* or Regent and named his able attendant Sonam Choephel as the first *Desi* to handle all political affairs. Gushri Khan and his Mongol troops stayed put in Tibet, spending the winters in Lhasa and the summers in the pasture lands of Dam, a little north of Lhasa. Though he did not interfere in the administration of Tibet, Gushri Khan and his army constituted an extra-legal and extraneous force which the Dalai Lama relied on to put down rebellions.

So, from the mid-seventeenth century onwards, the uniquely Tibetan theocracy of reincarnating Dalai Lamas ruling Tibet was established and the Dalai Lama became Tibet's uncontested supreme political and spiritual authority.

In keeping with his new majesty, the Fifth Dalai Lama encouraged visits by foreign envoys. In 1656, Shah Shuja, the Muslim ruler of Bengal, sent his envoys to the Fifth Dalai Lama. The new Sikkimese Chogyal paid a visit, and in 1643 the Malla kings of Nepal and the rulers of Ladakh sent envoys to Lhasa. So did other Indian rajahs. The kings of Mustang and Jumla, between whom the whole of the western part of modern Nepal was divided, came to Lhasa in person. But Bhutan, after Tibet's

failed military expeditions into the country, proved immune to Lhasa's new majesty.

In 1659, the Dalai Lama sent his representatives to Mongolia to ask the various Mongol tribal chieftains to remain united instead of constantly feuding with each other. The Manchu emperor, K'angsi, approached the Dalai Lama to obtain the assistance of Mongol and Tibetan troops to

quell a rebellion which he faced. However, the Dalai Lama refused to accede to the Emperor's request. He cited the hot climate of China as being unsuitable for the fighting capabilities of the Mongol and Tibetan troops. Around the same time the Dalai Lama received envoys from a dissident minister of the Manchu emperor who came to seek his support. The Dalai

✿ *A party at an aristocrat's mansion. Tibetans, aristocrats and commoners liked to picnic on the banks of the Kyichi river in Lhasa.*

Lama gave the same response but simultaneously sent a representative to Mongolia again to seek reconfirmation of Mongol unity in the event of civil strife breaking out in China.

Earlier the Dalai Lama had paid a visit to Peking at the invitation of Emperor Shun-chih who treated him with respect and equality. Manchu China had a vested interest in keeping the Dalai Lama happy because of his enormous spiritual influence in Mongolia, where the Mongols' passionate devotion to the Dalai Lama was matched by their occasional restlessness to disrupt the stability of the Middle Kingdom. Whatever later Chinese official historians chose to read into this visit, the meeting was clearly one between equals. Flinging the protocol of his new position aside, the Manchu emperor was prepared to go to the border of his domain and was prepared to receive the Tibetan potentate. But this was not the first contact between the Gelug hierarchy and the Manchus. In 1640 all the parties involved in the Tibetan power struggle—the Dalai Lama, his patron Gushri Khan, the Tsangpa king and his religious ally, the Karmapa—had sent representations to the Manchu court to seek the support of the rising power in Asia. At the time the Manchus were not rulers of China, but in 1664, they ousted the moribund Ming dynasty and ascended the celestial throne, the first non-Chinese dynasty to do so after the Mongols.

principles through the exercise of his secular power, surrounded by hard-headed politicians and pragmatic advisors, he maintained a reputation for religious tolerance and political broad-mindedness at a time when such qualities were being severely tested. He gave Tibet peace, prosperity and the greatly consolidated institution of the Dalai Lama. Later, the Tibetans attributed the wisdom of the Buddha, the glories of the ancient Tibetan emperors and the compassion of Avalokitesvara, the Protector of the Land of Snow, to the person of this Dalai Lama. Since then the Tibetans referred to this Dalai Lama as the Great Fifth.

Though the Fifth Dalai Lama laid the foundation for a solid Tibetan nation-state, his connections with the Mongols contributed to Tibet's later troubled history and undermined the very edifice he tried to set up.

Sangye Gyatso, the *Desi* of the Fifth Dalai Lama's last years, blacked out the news of his death and ruled in his stead till he was able to complete the construction of the Potala which was achieved in 1695. The *Desi* eventually recognised Tsangyang Gyatso as the Sixth Dalai Lama; the latter was well into his teens and his character and habits were already formed. He was enthroned in 1697, but his wayward, loose ways and his love for women and wine estranged him from Lhasang Khan, the grandson of Gushri Khan. Lhasang Khan

Meanwhile Gushri Khan died at the age of seventy-three and his two sons divided the realm of Qoshot power. Tashi Batur took the Kokonor region and Tenzin Dayan Khan remained in central Tibet.

In 1645 the Dalai Lama laid the foundation for the construction of the Potala Palace on the ruins of a palace built by Emperor Songtsen Gampo around 636. The Potala Palace, the apogee of a new spirit in Tibetan architecture, came to symbolise and dominate Lhasa and Tibet.

The Fifth Dalai Lama ushered Tibet into a golden age. Though he had to constantly compromise his spiritual sensibilities and

☼ *Devotees catch a glimpse of His Holiness as he passes by. Seeing His Holiness the Dalai Lama, provides immense spiritual satisfaction to Tibetan Buddhists.*

moved against the *Desi* who put up a stiff resistance but was overwhelmed by the superior Mongol power. The *Desi* was captured and killed and the Sixth Dalai Lama deposed. The Mongol cavalrymen took the Sixth Dalai Lama to the Kokonor region where, it is rumoured, he was killed. Lhasang Khan then installed a twenty-five-year-old monk, who was considered his natural son, as the real Dalai Lama. This sacrilege stiffened Tibetan opposition to their erstwhile protector and the Tibetans called in the Dzungars, a western Mongol tribe, for help.

Lhasang Khan was killed in an engagement with the Dzungars, while the Tibetans discovered the reincarnation of the Sixth Dalai Lama in Lithang in eastern Tibet. But selecting the Dzungars as their protector was unfortunate. Manchu China saw the Dzungars as potential rivals, not least because of their dealings with the Chinese rebel Wu Shih-pan who was trying to win Mongol support against the Manchu dynasty.

Manchu China was also worried by the increasing Dzungar military successes along the fringe of its empire. In his book, *The Search for Modern China,* Jonathan D. Spence writes: 'Under the brilliant leadership of Galdan, and drawing added unity from their deep devotion to the Dalai Lama in Tibet (whom they regarded as

✿ *A scene in front of the Buddhist School of Dialectics in Dharamsala. Forty years after being forced into exile in 1959, the Tibetans continue to cling to the dream of returning to a free Tibet.*

their spiritual leader), the Dzungars had been roaming at will over the largely unsettled lands known as Outer Mongolia and Qinghai. In the late 1670s, by seizing Kashgar, Hami and Turfan in turn, Galdan imposed his rule over the largely Muslim inhabitants of those cities and over their prosperous caravan routes linking China with the Mediterranean. The tribes, hostile to Galdan and defeated by him in battle, fled eastward, pressing the western Qing province of Gansu. This massive migration of warriors deeply worried the Emperor, who feared the possibility of a Russian-Dzungar alliance.'

Manchu China did not want the growing military might of the Dzungars sanctified by their close connection with the Dalai Lama. Manchu China feared the Dzungars might manipulate their closeness to the Gelug church of Tibet and the Mongols' devotion to the Dalai Lama to mobilise a united Mongolia behind them and challenge the Middle Kingdom. Impelled by these calculations, the Manchus moved into Tibetan politics.

As Jonathan Spence writes: 'But in foreign policy, each solution leads to a fresh problem. The power politics of the region were not resolved by Galdan's death, and Kangxi found himself drawn into complex struggles with other Dzungar leaders when the Dalai Lama was murdered, and an improperly chosen successor named in his place. This gave Kangxi the opportunity to invade Tibet in the name of righteous retribution (just as the Manchus had entered China in 1644); he despatched two armies, one of which entered Tibet through Kokonor, the other through the Sichuan province. In the autumn of 1720, the two armies joined forces in the Tibetan capital of Lhasa, and a new Dalai Lama, loyal to the Qing, was installed.'

Thus began the unhappy chapter of Manchu and later republican and communist China's active interference in the politics of Tibet.

✧ *The gilded and richly decorated image of Jowo, or the Buddha, in Jokhang in Lhasa.*
*FACING PAGE: His Holiness the Dalai Lama performs Tibetan New Year rituals on the rooftop of the main temple in Dharamsala.*

But before the entry of the Manchu forces into Lhasa, Phola, an able Tibetan leader who was a deputy of Lhasang Khan, reorganised the Tibetan army and drove the Dzungars out. The Manchu forces then entered Lhasa with the Seventh Dalai Lama, Kelsang Gyatso, who was installed in 1720. The Seventh Dalai Lama was a great scholar and did not involve himself in the administration of Tibet, though he did abolish the post of *Desi* and institute a council of ministers called the *kashag,* an institution which still exists in the polity of the Tibetan exiles.

The Manchus stationed an *amban* (as the Chinese representative was called) in Tibet, whose function and status has remained a source of dispute between Tibet and China to this day. The Tibetans claimed that the *amban* was Manchu China's ambassador to Tibet, while the Chinese called him Tibet's viceroy. The Manchus also stationed two thousand troops in Lhasa; this caused an immediate shortage of foodstuff and contributed to increasing resentment against the protecting power. The troops were removed and one immediate effect was the upsurge of old rivalries which were reflected in a divided *kashag*. Phola emerged the winner in this new round of power politics and, with the backing of the Manchus, became the de facto ruler of Tibet. Under the rule of this administrator, Tibet had the luxury of enjoying twenty years of good and stable government.

David Snellgrove and Hugh Richardson write in *A Cultural History of Tibet:* 'It is a mark of Phola's greatness that although his supremacy involved the subordination and, at times, the exile of the Seventh Dalai Lama, he was able by his conciliatory and just behaviour to keep monastic resentment to a low level. In his relations with China he shrewdly saw that as long as Tibetan policy did not endanger the wider interests of China in central Asia, Chinese overlordship in Tibet could be reduced to a mere formality as far as internal matters and even Tibetan relations with her Himalayan neighbours were concerned. Thus the substance of Tibetan independence was preserved thanks to Chinese protection but without fear of Chinese interference. His success was complete; he won the full confidence of the Emperor by his competence and reliability, and in Lhasa his dealings with the *amban* were firm but friendly; so they remained little more than observers and diplomatic agents of their Emperor.'

But Phola's collaboration with the Manchus laid the groundwork for the Manchu and later the Chinese claim of overlordship of Tibet, a situation which his son tried to rectify hastily and unsuccessfully. On his father's death, Gurmey Namgyal Phola immediately tried to shake off the Manchu yoke. He failed. The Dalai Lama was restored to power with a new *kashag* of four ministers to assist him. After the death of the Seventh

✿ *The Buddha gave his first discourse here in Sarnath, northern India, one of the most sacred pilgrim spots for Buddhists the world over.*

Dalai Lama, Tibet entered into a period of regency.

At this point another fissure in the Tibetan polity came from Tashilhunpo in Shigatse, the spiritual seat of Tibet's Panchen Lamas. The Fifth Dalai Lama had handed over the monastery of Tashilhunpo to his teacher, Choekyi Gyaltsen, a much-respected religious figure, and announced that his teacher would seek rebirth in the same pattern as the Dalai Lamas in a line of boy-successors. Thus the Fifth Dalai Lama's tutor had become the First Panchen Lama or The Great Scholar. The Manchus tried to patronise the institution of the Panchen Lamas as a

This period gave the Gelug church, though not necessarily the Dalai Lamas, the opportunity to continue to consolidate its power and influence in Tibet. The Buddhist church totally dominated Tibetan politics, and attempts by secular forces to wrest the power of governance came to nought.

David Snellgrove and Hugh Richardson state in *A Cultural History of Tibet:* 'Thus from 1757 onwards there came a period of 130 years during which the head of the administration was a Gelug lama regent, assisted by monk officials of his order and lay officials of the Gelugpa nobility. The Eighth Dalai Lama lived to the age of forty-seven, but he was disinclined to worldly affairs. After him four Dalai Lamas all died young, at the ages of ten, twenty-one, seventeen and twenty. There is good reason to believe that the Tenth Dalai Lama was assassinated, with the connivance of the then regent. Western writers have also expressed suspicions about the early death of the others, which resulted in power remaining in the hands of some dignitary of the Gelug "church", but that is not supported by anything in Tibetan or Chinese records or by Tibetan oral tradition. Whatever the truth may be, this rule of regents produced considerable variety of character. Some were revered and peaceful, while others were harsh and unscrupulous. In the main, the country remained peaceful and the regents remarkably free of Chinese control.'

counterbalancing force within the Gelug church, which constituted the same old story of 'Divide and Rule'; it once again set the province of U against Tsang, and the Dalai Lama against the Panchen Lama.

After the death of the Seventh Dalai Lama, Tibet stepped into a period of seclusion and self-imposed isolation. At the time the British were consolidating their power in India; the Manchus, the other great power in Asia, were on the decline. Racked by internal rebellion and a resurgent West pounding at its front door, the Manchus were hardly able to maintain their earlier influence in Tibet. This suited the Tibetans and their ruling elite just fine.

*FOLLOWING PAGES 48-49:*
*The square in front of the main temple in McLeod Ganj, Dharamsala, where all the important cultural and political events are held. The square once hosted an international concert for Tibet, attracting rock bands, singers and artistes from the United States, South Africa, Norway, as well as Indians like Ustad Zakir Hussain and Pandit Shiv Shankar.*

# CHAPTER 3

# God-Kings of the
# MODERN WORLD

Thubten Gyatso, the Great Thirteenth Dalai Lama, was born in 1876 in Dagpo in southern Tibet. He was enthroned with full powers in 1895 and managed to survive an assassination attempt early on in his reign. He ruled Tibet firmly and justly by hard work and astute political sense over a period which coincided with Tibet's innocent brush with international politics and the 'great game' which British India and Czarist Russia were playing in Central Asia and beyond.

In 1904, Lord Curzon, the Viceroy of India, suspecting Russian intentions in

*FACING PAGE: The Great Thirteenth Dalai Lama who safeguarded Tibet's independence.*

Tibet, despatched Colonel Younghusband to Tibet. Slaughtering around two thousand irregulars who were armed with broadswords at Guru, and overcoming a half-hearted Tibetan resistance at the desolate town of Gyantse, the British troops with Sikh and Gorkha regiments, marched on to Lhasa to prick what some colonial commentators called 'that bloated bubble of monkish power'.

The Thirteenth Dalai Lama, only twenty-eight, fled to Mongolia, leaving the abbot of Gaden monastery as his regent to negotiate on his behalf. The *amban* issued

a proclamation deposing the Dalai Lama but people smeared the edict with manure.

Younghusband made a deal with the Tibetans. The treaty signed between Tibet and British India in Lhasa in September 1904 required Tibet to recognise Britain as protector of Sikkim; to promote trade with India, to accept the opening of three British trade marts in Tibet and to prevent other foreigners exercising influence in Tibet—a clear reference to Russia. This treaty was an attempt by Britain to convert Tibet into a vast buffer, dividing the three main powers of the day.

While in Mongolia, the Dalai Lama turned his attention to Russia. He established contacts with the court in St. Petersburg through his emissary Dorjieff, a

*✿ A retinue of high lamas and their retainers. In old Tibet the best transport was either the horse or yak. Aristocrats and high lamas used brightly decorated horses as their means of transport.*

Buriat monk, who had studied in Lhasa and managed to gain the confidence of the Tibetan pontiff. But Russia had just lost the disastrous Russo-Japanese war and was in no position to offer Tibet any assistance against the British.

According to *A History of Modern Tibet* by Melvyn C. Goldstein, the Dalai Lama then changed his strategy and pursued two new courses of action. He sought accommodation with the Chinese who had deposed him in 1904. At the same time he decided it was important to improve relations with the British who controlled India.

Goldstein continues: 'With regard to the former, he appears to have instructed his regent in Tibet to ask the *amban* in

Lhasa to request the Manchu emperor to invite him to Peking so that he could explain the real situation in Tibet. With regard to the latter, he reinstated Shatra, Sholkhang and Changkyim—the three *shapes* (ministers) who had been dismissed in 1903 for being pro-British, promoting each to the position of *lonchen* (prime minister) with authority over the *kashag.'*

The Dalai Lama spent a year in Amdo. There he received the invitation to visit the Emperor in Peking. He arrived in Peking on September 28, 1908—the first Dalai Lama to do so since the Great Fifth.

The Dalai Lama was received at the imperial court with respect. However, Chinese protocol was designed to give the impression that the Dalai Lama was the leader of a vassal state. This treatment was in marked contrast to the reception given to the Fifth Dalai Lama who was received as the ruler of an independent country. However, titles were exchanged between the Dalai Lama and the Emperor. The Dalai Lama also took the opportunity to contact the British, French, American, German and Russian embassies.

This visit was used by the Manchu court to demonstrate the subordination of Tibet to the Manchus. In fact, some commentators described the Dalai Lama's visit to Peking as surrendering his temporal rule to China. William Rockhill, the American ambassador to China, wrote to

his President: 'The special interest to me is that I have probably been a witness to the overthrow of the temporal power of the Head of the Yellow Church.'

This sentiment was echoed by a reporter for *The Times* in London, who while all praise for the behaviour of the officials accompanying the Dalai Lama, thought that the Tibetan pontiff's political rule was over. He wrote: 'During the stay of the Dalai Lama in Peking, the demeanour of his followers has been excellent, and has given no ground for the outrageous stories of misconduct, nor any justification for such epithets as "barbarian hordes", applied to them by certain European newspapers. His visit has coincided with the end of his temporal power, but he has been treated with dignity befitting his spiritual office.'

But these observers underestimated the Thirteenth Dalai Lama's staying power and his growing political skills.

✿ *Representatives of British India, Republican China and Tibet meet in Simla (1913-1914) to demarcate Tibet's border with India and China.*

Meanwhile in Peking, the young emperor and the dowager empress, the power behind the declining Manchu court, suddenly died. The Dalai Lama performed the last rites.

Having received some measure of assurance from the Manchu court, the Dalai Lama then returned to Tibet. He arrived in Lhasa in 1909, after five years of absence. Two months later, two thousand Chinese troops followed and camped within striking distance of the city. An advance force marched on Lhasa, firing on the people and poised to capture the Dalai Lama and his ministers. But the Dalai Lama and his ministers managed to escape—this time to India. The Chinese *amban* issued an edict deposing the Dalai Lama again; the response from Lhasa's citizens was the same. They smeared the edict with Tibet's choicest yak dung. The *amban* tried to install the Panchen Lama as Tibet's spiritual and political leader in the

Dalai Lama's place. The Panchen Lama refused to oblige.

The British invasion of Tibet in 1904 had alerted Manchu China to the reality that Tibet was China's back door. If China was not able to secure Tibet, the Middle Kingdom would be vulnerable to future British ambitions. This was the main reason for China's sudden reversal of policy towards Tibet.

The Dalai Lama and his party fled to Dromo, crossed Sikkim to Kalimpong and eventually made their way to Darjeeling. There Sir Charles Bell, the British political officer to Sikkim, Bhutan and Tibet, met and hosted the Tibetan leader.

In his book, *A Portrait of the Dalai Lama: The Life and Times of the Great Thirteenth*, Sir Charles Bell describes his first encounter with the most important pontiff of central Asia. 'The Dalai Lama was thirty-four years old when I met him in Darjeeling... was about five feet, six inches in height, and therefore a little below the Tibetan average. His complexion was a darker hue of one of humble birth. The nose was slightly aquiline. The large well-set ears were a sign that he was an incarnation of Chenrezig... His dark-brown eyes were large and very prominent. They lit up as he spoke or listened, and his whole countenance shone with quiet eagerness.

'There were several people present in the room when I entered, but as soon as

the Dalai Lama began to tell me why he had to fly to India, all those present, including the Crown Prince of Sikkim, left the audience chamber, leaving me alone with His Holiness.

'We spoke in the Tibetan of the Lhasa dialect, which is of all the most highly esteemed.'

The Dalai Lama told Sir Charles Bell: 'I have come to India to ask the help of the British government against the Chinese. Unless they intervene, China will occupy Tibet and oppress it; she will destroy the Buddhist religion there and the Tibetan Government, and will govern the country through Chinese officials. Eventually her power will be extended into States on the border between Tibet and India.'

The Dalai Lama travelled to Calcutta and met the Viceroy, Lord Minto, and reiterated his request for British assistance to expel the Chinese troops from Tibet. But British India decided neutrality was the best policy. In short, Britain was willing to give China complete control of Tibet, while insisting that China must not interfere in Nepal, Sikkim and Bhutan.

However, as soon as China had consolidated its position in Tibet, the Chinese government claimed both Nepal and Bhutan as feudatory states. The Bhutanese ruler had permitted several Tibetan officials to stay in Bhutan. The

Chinese *amban* in Lhasa demanded an explanation for this. He also demanded that Bhutan use as its currency, the coins that the *amban* was circulating in Tibet.

However, the British, despite their calculated policy of neutrality, were not unaware of the enormous influence of the Dalai Lama. Sir Charles Bell wrote: 'Indeed, his influence extended not only over Tibet, but also over Mongolia, parts of China, the large tract east of Lake Baikal in Siberia which was inhabited by the Buryiat Mongols, and even districts in European Russia, peopled by the Torgots and other Mongol tribes. As regards the

*✿ The square in front of Jokhang in Lhasa, with a scattering of worshippers and pilgrims.*
*FACING PAGE: A demonstration to remember those who died in the 1959 uprising against Chinese rule.*

Manchus, it was only the older ones who were Buddhists and looked with reverence on the Dalai Lama. The younger generation was greatly under Chinese and European influence and consequently lost faith in him. The Manchus seldom came to Lhasa. The Russian Consulate in India assured me that the Russian Government owed much to the Dalai Lama, for the latter's adherents were among the most law-abiding of the Tsar's subjects.'

In 1911 the tide turned in Tibet's favour. A revolution broke out in China and the Ch'ing Dynasty was overthrown. Racked by corruption, rebellions and

imperialism, Manchu China had found it increasingly difficult to control its vast empire. Rallying around the cry 'Down with foreign Manchu rule', the Chinese people, led by the great revolutionary, Dr Sun Yat-sen, gave the final push to a collapsing imperial structure. China became a republic controlling some key cities, while the rest of the country was ruled by rival warlords.

'So . . . more than two millennia of China were brought to a close. And with almost no experience whatsoever in the arts and institutions of self-government, the Chinese people were presented with the option of devising their own future in a watchful and dangerous world,' writes Jonathan Spence in

✿ *Dark days for Tibet: A gompa being used as a stable in Tsaparong, western Tibet.*

*The Search for Modern China.*

In Tibet the stranded Chinese troops mutinied, looted the *amban's* residence and held him captive. The marauding Chinese soldiers were overpowered by the Tibetan army and expelled from Tibet to China through India. The present scattered Chinese families in Darjeeling and Kalimpong, and the residents of Calcutta's Chinatown are the descendants of those Chinese soldiers who decided to remain in India rather than face an uncertain future in a chaotic China.

The Dalai Lama made his triumphant return to Tibet in 1912 and reached Lhasa in January 1913 to a rapturous welcome. He issued a proclamation of Tibetan

independence and letters to this effect were sent to various governments. Yuan Shih-kai, the first President of the young Chinese republic, sent the Dalai Lama a telegram in which he stated that the Tibetan leader's power was restored. The Dalai Lama replied that he had not asked for his rank and authority from the Chinese government and stated bluntly that with or without Chinese approval, he intended to exercise both political and spiritual authority in Tibet.

But Tibet's problem with China did not end with the Dalai Lama's return to his country. Despite Sun Yat-sen's recommendation that the non-Chinese should decide whether they wished to

*☼ A Tibetan being led away by the police—a familiar scene in Chinese-occupied Tibet.*

remain in China or secede, Yuan Shih-kai's government, nervous of Britain's growing influence in Tibet, decided to grab as much Tibetan territory as it could. Areas in Kham in eastern Tibet like Batang, Chamdo, Drayab, Markham and others were retaken by republican Chinese forces. In 1913 the Chinese forces overran Chatreng and started to push westward. The Dalai Lama appointed Chamba Tendar as the Governor-General of Kham and sent him to the region with a reinvigorated Tibetan army. The Governor-General raised a local Khamba militia. This enlarged Tibetan force managed to push the Chinese army from Shopando, Lho Dzong and Khyungpo and established defensive positions along the line of the divide of the Salween and Mekong rivers.

British India and an independent Tibet saw that it was vital to tie down China in a formal treaty so that it would have no choice but to guarantee peace and stability on Tibet's volatile eastern frontier. The British managed to persuade China to participate in talks held in Simla, which were attended by representatives of Tibet and British India.

Lochen (Prime Minister) Shatra, the Tibetan representative to the tripartite conference in Simla, stated the Tibetan case: 'Tibet and China have never been under each other and will never associate with each other in the future. It is decided that Tibet is an independent State and that the Precious Protector, the Dalai Lama, is the ruler of Tibet, in all temporal as well as spiritual affairs.'

But in the end Tibet was forced to accept the points contained in the Simla Convention of 1914. The country was to be divided into Outer and Inner Tibet, along the lines of Mongolia. Outer Tibet would remain effectively under the rule of the Dalai Lama, though under nominal Chinese suzerainty. Within the latter zone, China was accorded the right to establish a measure of control but without in any way infringing the integrity of Tibet as a geographical and political entity.

But though Ivan Chen, the Chinese representative, put his initials on the agreement, he refused to sign it. This led

☼ *The Potala Palace, the winter residence of Tibet's Dalai Lama, was first built in 700 A.D. by King Songtsen Gompo but assumed its present shape during the reign of the Fifth Dalai Lama.*

Sir Henry McMahon, the British representative and the Secretary of State of the Government of India, to issue the following warning: 'As it is, the patience of His Majesty's Government is exhausted and they have no alternative but to inform the Chinese Government that, unless the Convention is signed before the end of the month, they will hold themselves free to sign separately with Tibet.

'In that case the Chinese Government will, of course, lose all the privileges and advantages which the tripartite convention secures for them, including recognition of Chinese suzerainty over Tibet.'

Tibet went ahead with signing a bilateral agreement with Britain on July 3, 1914. The agreement contained a formal declaration which stated that as long as China withheld signature of the agreement, it would be debarred from exercising any rights contained in the agreement.

British India came out the winner in this strange diplomatic game. Britain secured Tibet as a friendly neighbour, obtained favourable trade terms with Tibet and secured present-day Arunachal Pradesh in return for the promise of an arms' supply to Tibet. Tibet's position remained as before. Tibet and China were still at war and Tibet received no mutually-agreed-upon guarantee from China regarding its political status.

Instead China's ambitions regarding Tibet grew. In 1918 General Peng Ri-shing, the newly appointed commander of south-west China, advanced into Tibetan territory for a full-scale invasion. He rejected Tibetan attempts at conciliation. But the Tibetan troops were better trained than before. They crossed the Mekong river and drove back the invading Chinese forces. After months of fighting, General Peng surrendered and three thousand Chinese soldiers were captured and sent to Lhasa to be repatriated to China through India. This added to the population of Calcutta's Chinatown. Tibetan troops recaptured a great deal of Tibetan territory that Chinese troops had held since 1910. Eric Teichman, the British consular officer in Dartsedo said: 'Another month or two would possibly have seen several thousand more Chinese prisoners in Tibetan hands and the Lhasa forces in possession of all the country up to Ta Chien-lu.' Dartsedo is the farthest point of Tibetan territory, not far from Chengdu, the capital of Sichuan province. The Chinese refer to it as Kanting today but in those days it was called by its sinicised name, Ta Chien-lu.

At this point the Chinese called on the British to intervene. Eric Teichman was deputed as the chief mediator. A peace

treaty was signed but it was never ratified by Peking. However, both parties respected the provisions of the treaty for the next twelve years and Lhasa remained in control of most of the newly recovered territories till 1949 when communist China invaded Tibet.

Despite constant incursions of Chinese troops into Tibet throughout his reign, the Dalai Lama, by sheer force of his personality, was able to give Tibet a measure of peace and social stability. Though he was continually concerned about Tibet's status vis-a-vis China, the uneasy truce with its large eastern neighbour gave the Dalai Lama some breathing space and he was able to turn his attention to the development and modernisation of Tibet. The Dalai Lama's experiences of exile in China and India widened his horizons, and he was convinced that in order to survive, Tibet had to break its isolationist policy and open its doors to the changes sweeping the rest of the world.

The Dalai Lama established a postal system on modern lines and constructed a mint which produced Tibet's first paper currency. He modernised and enlarged the Tibetan army, sent four students to England to receive a modern education, established English schools in Lhasa and Gyantse and permitted the members of the

*☼ Long walk to freedom— the Dalai Lama on his way to India.*
*FACING PAGE: His Holiness being greeted by an Indian official at an army outpost on the border between the North-East Frontier Agency and Assam.*

aristocracy and the middle class to send their children to English schools in Darjeeling and Kalimpong. He built Tibet's first power station which supplied electricity to Lhasa. Motorable roads were built and he was the proud owner of Tibet's first car, a Baby Austin, Tibet No. 1. The Dalai Lama's favourite attendant Chensel Kunphel-la drove Tibet No. 2. The Dalai Lama also set up Tibet's first police force, which operated only in the city of Lhasa, and the first telegraph line linking Lhasa with Gyantse and India was opened.

In addition, the Dalai Lama did much to improve Tibet's law and order. He increased his own contact with ordinary people and introduced more merciful standards into the administration of justice while reducing monastic domination of Tibet's political affairs.

Many of his predecessors had been weak personalities or had died too young to exercise any meaningful authority. However, endowed with a forceful character and strong will-power, the Thirteenth Dalai Lama recaptured for the institution of the Dalai Lama, the authority and power which the Great Fifth had given it. Due to his efforts the institution of the Dalai Lama was increasingly identified with the survival of the Tibetan nation-state. Like the Fifth, the Thirteenth Dalai Lama is referred to by Tibetans as the Great Thirteenth, a measure of the people's gratitude for his untiring efforts to give Tibet a degree of international identity.

Shortly before his death in 1933, the Thirteenth Dalai Lama issued what has come to be called his Political Testament, which, in hindsight, constitutes an uncanny prophecy of the fate that awaited Tibet. In this, he urged the Tibetan people to work for the good of Tibet. Otherwise, he warned: 'It may happen that here in the centre of Tibet, the religion and the secular administration may be attacked both from the outside and from the inside. Unless we

*His Holiness and entourage at the border of India in 1959.*

can guard our country, it will now happen that the Dalai and the Panchen Lamas, the Father and the Son, the holders of the faith, the glorious rebirths, will be broken down and left without a name. As regards the monasteries and monks and nuns, their lands and other properties will be destroyed. The administrative customs of the Three Religious Kings will be weakened. The officers of the state, ecclesiastical and secular, will find their

of representatives of British India, China, Nepal, Bhutan and Sikkim. He assumed both political and spiritual authority of Tibet in 1950, at the age of fifteen—the youngest Dalai Lama to do so. That year communist China's Red Army, flushed with victory in the Chinese civil war, overran Chamdo and was on the verge of advancing into Lhasa. The spirited fight put up by the poorly-equipped Tibetan army was easily brushed aside by the People's Liberation Army. Tibet's plea for help to India, Britain, the United States and Nepal went unheeded. Diplomatically isolated, Tibet had no alternative except to sign a 17-point treaty with China in 1951, in which Tibet agreed to form a part of the motherland. From 1951 to 1959 Buddhist Tibet co-existed with communist China. However, China broke all the promises it made in the 17-point treaty and started a campaign of repression in Amdo and Kham. Tibetan resistance grew, culminating in a major uprising in Lhasa in 1959. The movement was easily quelled by the Chinese army and the Dalai Lama fled to India, followed by thousands of Tibetans.

China might have thought that with the Dalai Lama gone, the problem of Tibet was solved once and for all. But then China forgot the enormous spiritual authority enjoyed by Tibet's Dalai Lama. Rajmohan Gandhi, the grandson of Mahatma Gandhi, considers the present Dalai Lama as 'Providence's gift to Tibet and Tibet's gift

lands seized and their other property confiscated, and they themselves made to serve their enemies, or wander about the country as beggars. All beings will be sunk in great hardship and in overpowering fear.'

The Fourteenth Dalai Lama was discovered in Amdo, the north-eastern province along Tibet's contested borders with China. He was brought to Lhasa in 1939 and on February 22, 1940, he ascended the Lion Throne in the presence to the world. If persons across the earth know and respect him, it is due to events (including painful events) and to his personal traits. Those who made it necessary for him to go into exile did not know that they would supply a remarkable figure to the world's stage!'

B y going into exile the Dalai Lama lost a country but has managed to create an empire. There are numerous reasons for the increasing pervasiveness of the Tibetan issue on the international forum. There is the David versus Goliath confrontation: a weak Tibet pitted against an increasingly powerful China. Then there is the growing appeal of Tibetan Buddhism in the West which has sensitised Western ears to the Tibetans' political message. There is also the captivating personality of the Dalai Lama who has emerged as a global figure and whose views on the issues of the day are listened to with respect. The collapse of communism in traditional Buddhist nations and areas like Mongolia, Tuva, Buryatia and Kalmykia, where the belief in the Dalai Lama has outlived the brutality of the communist rule, has enormously expanded the Dalai Lama's parish.

In fact, by fleeing their isolated but occupied homeland, the Tibetans merely did not travel to another country but fast-forwarded themselves to the twentieth century. It is a measure of the Tibetans'

*His Holiness the Dalai Lama, the Panchen Lama and Chou En-lai, the Chinese premier, in Beijing in 1954.*

resilience and the wisdom of the Dalai Lama that in the rough and tumble of India's plural political culture, the Tibetan exiles decided to shed their medieval political trappings and transform their community into a vibrant democracy based on the belief that this would be replicated in a self-governing, democratic Tibet.

One of the accomplishments of the Dalai Lama is the creation of a cohesive, highly educated community in exile, passionately dedicated to the cause of freeing their compatriots from the yoke of communist oppression. He set up eleven major agricultural settlements in south India for the rehabilitation of Tibetan refugees, eighty-five residential schools, a university, health clinics, monasteries, cultural institutions and commercial enterprises—all with the assistance of the Indian government. He formed a small but effective bureaucracy to manage this interlocking network of institutions and established a parliament where the refugees could have a say in the affairs of the community.

Franz Michael, the author of *Rule by Reincarnation: Tibetan Buddhism and Its Role in Society and State,* makes these

*FACING PAGE: Destroyed monasteries and communities in Tibet re-appear in India. PAGES 70-71: A resurgent monastic community provides a strong support to the Tibetan exiles.*

comments on the Tibetan refugee community: 'The survival of Tibetan culture in the Indian diaspora is one of the wondrous and hopeful events of our time... When His Holiness the Dalai Lama arrived in India after his incredible escape from Lhasa over the high Himalayan mountain passes, followed by tens of thousands of exhausted, sick and destitute Tibetan men, women and children, seeking refuge from Chinese terror after their futile uprising against the foreign invader, few would have thought that here was the core for the continuance of an abiding, indeed, advancing great culture. Yet the Tibetan story is an outstanding example of what faith and loyalty to one's culture can accomplish in gaining under a great leadership—an almost miraculous recovery from a grievous, seemingly disastrous blow. In India, the Tibetan polity, its settlements, its enterprises and its religio-political structure have not only flourished but have transformed and developed from the prototype in Tibet into an active part of the modern world.'

The Fourteenth Dalai Lama has managed to transform a medieval Central Asian institution into a positive force with global importance in this age.

# Thirteen Dalai Lamas:
# A RETROSPECTIVE

From 1391 to 1933, thirteen Dalai Lamas held sway over the Tibetan populace. Two, however, the Fifth and the Thirteenth Dalai Lamas, were singled out to go down in history with the added title, 'Great'.

## GEDUN DRUB
### The First Dalai Lama

The First Dalai Lama, Gedun Drub, was born Pema Dorje in 1391 at Gyurmey Rupa, near Sakya in the Tsang region of central Tibet to Gonpo Dorje and Jomo Namkha Kyi, a nomadic family.

☼ *FACING PAGE: Monks scramble for pills and strings blessed by His Holiness the Dalai Lama.*

According to *The Biography of the All-Knowing Gedun Drub*, written by Yeshi Tsemo and published in 1494, Pema Dorje was fair-complexioned with a parasol-shaped head, a big protuberant forehead, an aquiline nose, long ear-lobes, and graced with a pair of the clearest, sharpest eyes.

The night Pema Dorje was born, disaster struck his family. Brigands, the plague of Tibet's nomadic grasslands, raided his parents' tent. His parents managed to hide their newborn baby among the nearby rocks, before being taken captive by the rampaging brigands.

The next morning the family's granny came looking for the baby, fearful whether he was even alive. She spotted a crow, its wings fully spread to protect the baby. Astounded by this unusual scene, the old woman remarked to the bird: 'I can't say that you are a protective spirit, because you wouldn't have let the robbers raid our tent and ravish his mother. But I can't also say that you are a malignant spirit, because otherwise you wouldn't be protecting this helpless newborn.' With this she took the baby in her weak and trembling arms and walked away.

Pema Dorje was later reunited with his parents. The raid of the brigands had reduced his parents to poverty and they took to begging. Unable to support Pema Dorje, and in the hope that he would have a better life, Gonpo Dorje and Jomo Namkha Kyi gave away their son to a well-to-do family in the area to tend their herd of yaks and sheep. When tending his herd, Pema Dorje spontaneously started carving spiritual motifs on stones and rocks, some of which, it is said, can be seen to this day. There were other indications of his profoundly spiritual character early on in life. He was reputed to have told his parents and friends that he remembered his previous lives, right to the past hundred existences.

While looking after the rich family's herd, Pema Dorje also attended teachings

*Sprawling monasteries become the base for mass appeal for the Gelugs.*

given by sundry lamas, which shaped his attitude towards life. When he was fifteen years old, he told his companions that to cling to the worldly life and not follow the teachings of the Buddha was like living in a burning house.

Pema Dorje left his shepherding existence and joined Narthang monastery.

In 1405 he took his novice vows from Khenchen Drupa Sherab, abbot of Narthang, and assumed the religious name of Gedun Drub. Narthang monastery later became one of Tibet's finest printing houses. Around 1411 when he was 20, Gedun Drub took his vows of monkhood and became fully ordained.

The Tibet of Gedun Drub's youth was going through an unsettled period. The semblance of unity which the Sakyapas gave Tibet, with the persuasive military assistance of the Mongols, had dissipated. Tibet was once again divided by fractious rival forces, regional and political, jostling for national pre-eminence with the

Nyingma and the Kagyu schools of Tibetan Buddhism giving spiritual support to their political and worldly patrons. With the disappearance of Sakya dominance over Tibet, the struggle for supremacy was between the provincial warlords of Tsang and U. With its capital Lhasa, U, which means centre, had never forgotten that it was the starting point of the military expeditions which the Tibetan kings had launched since the seventh century and which had unified Tibet, enabling Tibetan power to extend to the heart of Asia and elsewhere.

Into this scene entered Tsongkapa who was born near Kumbum in Amdo at the very fringe of Tibet's border with China in the north-east. Tsongkapa was a great reformer and founded the Gelugpa school (the Virtuous Ones) of Tibetan Buddhism whose stress on celibacy and strict adherence to the discipline of the Buddhist monastic system attracted an enormous following and transformed it into a great spiritual force. And the well-spring of the growing spiritual prestige of the Gelugpa was centred on the monastery of Gaden, near Lhasa, which Tsongkapa founded and where he taught, wrote, meditated and supervised his growing monastic community according to traditional rules of monastic discipline.

Drawing on his eclectic spiritual education, and especially on the teachings of the great Indian priest, Atisha, Tsongkapa wrote the *Lamrim,* a full account of the path to enlightenment, which became a cornerstone of Gelugpa theology.

The young Gedun Drub was aware of the fame of Tsongkapa and that of his school. In 1416 he became a disciple of Tsongkapa and from that day, it is said, he followed his lama like a dog his master. His loyalty and devotion to Tsongkapa persuaded the great master to make Gedun Drub his principal disciple, bypassing such older disciples like the great scholar,

Gyaltsab Dharma Rinchen and the more famous Khedrub Je. Tsongkapa handed Gedun Drub a brand new set of robes as a gesture that he would spread the teachings of the Buddha all over Tibet. Some accounts also claim that Gedun Drub was, in fact, Tsongkapa's nephew.

Gedun Drub's contribution to the cause of the Gelugpa lay in his energy and ability in consolidating Tsongkapa's school and transforming it into an active and increasingly expansive order. In 1447 he founded the Tashilhunpo monastery in Shigatse, which then lay on the very edge of the territory dominated by the Ringpung who had the spiritual backing of the

school had devised and adopted, and which assured it a smooth and unbroken succession of spiritual leaders without having to go through disruptive and debilitating succession struggles.

In their book, *A Cultural History of Tibet,* David Snellgrove and Hugh Richardson noted: 'Appreciating the prestige which older sects had gained through the system of reincarnating lamas, Gedun Drub may well have arranged before his death that the same means of succession should be adopted by the Gelug. At all events, in due course a successor was found whose birth came sufficiently close to his death. Named Gedun Gyatso, this successor was treated subsequently as a reincarnation and regarded retrospectively as the second of the Dalai Lamas. Despite the mystique with which some Westerners like to regard the whole practice of reincarnating lamas, the custom was clearly adopted and maintained for reasons of statecraft.'

Gedun Drub was a person of immense scholarship, famous for combining study and practice, and wrote more than eight voluminous books on his insight into the Buddha's teachings and his philosophy. In addition he was in meditation retreat for over twenty years.

In 1474, at the age of eighty-four, Gedun Drub died while in meditation at Tashilhunpo, the monastery he had founded.

Karma Kagyu school of Tibetan Buddhism. With the establishment of such powerful monasteries, the Gelugpa, which remained on the periphery of the struggle for national dominance, became an important player in the shaping of Tibetan destiny by virtue of its expanding monastic community.

Gedun Drub's second important contribution to the Gelugpa's domination of all Tibet was his attraction to the system of reincarnating lamas which the Kagyu

✿ *The plaza in front of the Tsuglakhang in Lhasa, re-done by the Chinese rulers.*

## GEDUN GYATSO

### The Second Dalai Lama

Gedun Gyatso was born in 1476 at Tanak, near Shigatse, to Kunga Gyaltsen and Machik Kunga Pemo. His father was a well-known tantric master belonging to the Nyingma sect. When Gedun Gyatso was able to speak, he was reported to have told his parents that his name was Pema Dorje, the birth name of the First Dalai Lama, and that his father was Lobsang Drakpa, Tsongkapa's ordination name, and went on to explain the mannerisms of Tsongkapa when giving public teachings.

✿ *Monks return to their monastic quarters after their daily prayer ceremonies.*

When Gedun Gyatso was conceived, his father had a dream in which someone dressed in white appeared and told him to name his son Gedun Drub. The white apparition said that his son would be a person with the ability to recollect his past lives.

However, Kunga Gyaltsen named his son Sangye Phel. But sure enough, true to his dream, Gedun Gyatso had a computer-like memory, and he learned to read and write without anyone teaching him. However, he was a mischievous boy, always getting into trouble. One day, when

Gedun Gyatso graduated from merely being mischievous to being an outright nuisance, his mother gave him a severe tongue-lashing. A nonchalant Gedun Gyatso retorted, 'Don't scold me, but pray to me.'

'How should I pray to you?' his astonished mother asked.

'Like this,' Gedun Gyatso said and broke into a spontaneous song:

You, the wish-fulfilling gem,
Whose wisdom is acquired without study,
Who heard the teachings,
Meditated on them,
And having practised them
Became a realised being.
I pray to your unceasing
accomplishments.

His mother also had something poetic up her sleeve and told her son that she too was deserving of respect and prayer, and sang this song:

To the mother as ferocious as a fighting
dog,
I pray to the ferocious dog-like mother.
To the mother as frightening as a
wounded bear,
I pray to the frightening bear-like mother.
To the mother as mad as a raging tiger,
I pray to the raging tiger-like mother.

*The main assembly hall of Choni monastery in north-eastern Tibet. The central thangka painting depicts Tsongkapa, the founder of the Gelug school of Tibetan Buddhism.*

According to the biography of Gedun Gyatso this indicates that both his parents were people who were highly realised and well versed in the teachings of the Buddha.

When Gedun Gyatso reached the age of four, he told his parents that he would like to live in Tashilhunpo monastery where the living quarters were pleasant and where he had left a half-eaten candy. 'That's where I have my monks and where I left some incomplete statues.'

At the age of four or eight—depending on which history book you are reading—Gedun Gyatso was recognised as the reincarnation of Gedun Drub and was installed at Tashilhunpo monastery. He took his novice vows from Panchen Lungrig Gyatso in 1486 and his vows of ordained monk from Choje Choekyi Gyaltsen, who gave him the ordination name Gedun Gyatso. He studied at Tashilhunpo and Drepung monasteries. At Drepung he built his residence and named it Gaden Phodrang. When the Fifth Dalai Lama assumed temporal rule of Tibet, the government came to be referred to as the government of Gaden Phodrang.

Gedun Gyatso is reputed to have been the first mystic to discover the potential sacredness of Lake Lhamoi Latso, the famous 'Lake of Visions', about ninety miles south-east of Lhasa. It is said that the divine scenery and signs which led to the discovery of the Thirteenth and Fourteenth Dalai Lamas were reflected on the surface

✿ *Below the Potala used to be the Shol printing press, one of the handful of such wood-block presses in Tibet.*

of the lake. He established the Chokhorgyal monastery near the sacred lake.

In 1517 Gedun Gyatso became the abbot of Drepung monastery and in 1518 he revived the Monlam Chenmo, the Great Prayer Festival, and presided over the event with monks from Sera, Drepung and Gaden. In 1525, he became the abbot of Sera monastery.

Gedun Gyatso was deep in meditation when he died at the age of sixty-seven in 1542.

### SONAM GYATSO
#### The Third Dalai Lama

The Third Dalai Lama was born Ranu Sicho Pelzang in 1543 at Tolung, near Lhasa to Namgyal Drakpa and to Pelzom Bhuti, whose father, Wangchuk Rinpoche, was a well-known tantric practitioner.

When Ranu Sicho Pelzang was conceived, his mother Pelzom Bhuti had a dream in which she flew through a window and landed on a big tree. At the same time a *garuda* (a large vulture) perched on a branch of the tree, saying that it had come from Drepung. In his father's dream, a man appeared saying, 'I'm the throne-holder of Sakya. A great *rinpoche* will be born to you and you should make preparations.'

The parents of Ranu Sicho Pelzang had many children before him, but they had all died. To ward off any misfortune which might take away this child from them, Namgyal Drakpa and Pelzom Bhuti fed him on the milk of a white goat and named him Ranu Sicho Pelzang—'The prosperous one saved by goat's milk.'

There are many instances recorded in his biography which show that Ranu Sicho Pelzang considered himself, even at an early age, deserving of high respect and deep reverence. One day Sonam Drakpa Gyaltsen Pelsangpo, a Sakya prince, invited Ranu Sicho Pelzang's parents to his residence. Namgyal Drakpa told his son to offer a scarf and to prostrate before the Sakya prince. His son offered the prince his scarf but refused to prostrate, and when the prince extended his hand to bless the boy, he moved his head sideways to avoid being touched by the prince, and gave a look of severe disapproval. The prince said, 'In that case, you bless me.' And the boy reached up for the prince's head and touched his head with his own forehead.

Hearing of the boy's exceptional behaviour, people around Tolung came to receive his blessings—some out of

☼ *Every winter thousands of Tibetan refugees flock to Bodh Gaya, the place where the Buddha attained enlightenment.*

curiosity, others in genuine faith. One day, when he was three years old, relatives of a deceased Khamba monk came to his house and requested him to pray for the dead lama. 'May he be born in the abode of the Buddha Amitabha. May he attain enlightenment,' the boy prayed. Then the relatives asked the boy to say a prayer for the living. And Ranu Sicho Pelzang promptly said, 'May you suffer from no illness. May you live long.'

During winter months, when the bitter wind from the plains of Jangthang blew south over Tolung, Ranu Sicho Pelzang would try to fill the cracks in the windows with twigs from a broom to prevent the chilly draught from entering the house. During that time he was found singing:

Happy will I be if this house is the Gaden
Phodrang,
Happy will I be if my mind encompasses
the ocean of
the Buddha's teachings,
Happy will I be if I can generate the
precious inner-heat,
Happy will I be if the warmth of that
bonfire is within me.

Or he would be discovered reciting this prayer of heartfelt spiritual longings addressed to the goddess Palden Lhamo and other guardian deities of the Buddhist faith:

O, the queen of the three realms and
twenty-six constellations,

The time has come for you to perform
your acts of virtue.
O, you countless dharma protectors,
Support the fulfilment of my efforts.

In 1546 Ranu Sicho Pelzang was recognised by Neudong, the ruler of Tibet, as the reincarnation of Gedun Gyatso. His hair was cut, symbolising his renunciation of the world and a pointed yellow hat of the Gelugpa pontiff was presented to him. He assumed the name of Sonam Gyatso and was escorted to Drepung monastery in a grand procession. With the sound of

*☼ Tibetans must be one of the biggest consumers of butter in the world. They use butter for tea and with meals; the best quality is reserved to light lamps for gods and deities.*

trumpets and clashing of cymbals, with scarves and burning incense, thousands of people greeted him at Drepung. Sonam Gyatso was enthroned on the snow-lion throne in Drepung.

In 1552, Sonam Gyatso became the abbot of Drepung monastery and in 1558, the abbot of Sera. In 1574 he established the Kusho Dratsang Pende Lekshe Ling, which is now called the Namgyal monastery and serves as the Dalai Lama's private monastery. Its monks assist the Dalai Lama in his private religious ceremonies and prayers.

Then Sonam Gyatso made a portentous decision which contributed to transforming the Gelugpa from a purely religious to a political force. He accepted an invitation from the Tumed chieftain, Altan Khan, to visit Mongolia. Since the days of Genghis Khan and Kublai Khan, the Mongols had lacked a chieftain whose energy and leadership could reunite them. Altan Khan, in a way, filled that role because he was the most powerful chief among the tribes living along the borders of China.

When these two major players in Tibetan history first met in 1578 near Lake Kokonor, titles were exchanged. The grand lama of Tibet received Ta-lai, spelled Dalai in Western literature, and which in Mongolian means ocean, as does *gyatso* in Tibetan. So Sonam Gyatso became the Dalai Lama, the Ocean of Wisdom, and his two predecessors were retroactively known as the First and Second Dalai Lamas. In turn, the Dalai Lama conferred on Altan Khan the title of Brahma, the king of religion.

This was not the first Tibetan Buddhist inroad into the grasslands of Mongolia. In the thirteenth century the lamas of Sakya, Sakya Pandita and his descendants, converted Kublai Khan to Buddhism and in return, the Sakya lamas were given control of all Tibet. But the Third Dalai Lama, by his tireless missionary activities, put the entire military might of Mongolia at the service of the Gelug school of Tibetan Buddhism. At the insistence of the Third Dalai Lama, Altan Khan enforced a

✿ *A panoramic view of the main secretariat of the Central Tibetan Administration in Dharamsala.*

ban among the Mongols on blood sacrifice and ancestor worship. David Snellgrove and Hugh Richardson note in *A Cultural History of Tibet* that the Third Dalai Lama 'travelled not only through those parts of Mongolia which were under the authority of the Genghizide Khans, but also within the Oirat confederacy, establishing a new "religious empire" outside of Tibet of such size and potential importance that it is not surprising that the Chinese emperor was anxious to invite him to Peking...'

## YONTEN GYATSO

### The Fourth Dalai Lama

The Fourth Dalai Lama was born in 1589 (on the thirtieth day of the twelfth month of the Earth-Ox year of the Tibetan calendar) in Mongolia to the Chokur tribal chieftain who was the grandson of Altan Khan.

Eight months after he was conceived, a white figure appeared in the boy's father's dream and told him: 'The boy is the reincarnation of the Dalai Lama. Put him on the throne. Let the public receive his blessings.'

In Tibet itself, Nechung, the state oracle of Tibet, proclaimed that the reincarnation would be born in Mongolia and Lamo Tsangpa, another oracle consulted by Tibetans, made the same prediction.

Around the same time, Tsultrim Gyatso, the chief attendant of the Third Dalai Lama, was living in Mongolia. He sent a letter to the authorities in Tibet saying that the reincarnation of the Dalai Lama had been born in Mongolia, giving details of the dreams of the father, and saying that on the morning of the birth, the whole neighbourhood had heard heavenly music punctuated by a minor tremor.

When the Fourth Dalai Lama was still a child, he was reported to have slept for three days and nights. When he finally awoke, his mother, in utter astonishment,

The Third Dalai Lama accepted the invitation and would have travelled to Peking but for his death while teaching in Mongolia in 1588. Besides travelling to Mongolia, the Third Dalai Lama also visited the Tibetan areas bordering China. In Tsongkapa's birthplace, he founded Kumbum monastery and the sprawling Lithang monastery in Kham. He also converted the powerful Nashi tribes between Tibet and China in the south-east to the Gelug order.

asked him why he had slept for so long. The boy said that he had had a great dream. On the first day, he dreamt that he had taken the family's butter lamp from the altar and held it high. The radiance of the lamp grew brighter and brighter until it illuminated the whole world. On the second day, he dreamt that he saw the sky filled with an enormous rainbow under which sat countless numbers of Buddhas and Bodhisattvas. On the third day the boy dreamt that he rose from this throne, studded with precious stones, and walked towards Tibet.

*Norbulingka or the Jewel Park, the summer residence of the Dalai Lamas built by the Seventh Dalai Lama.*

The principal lamas of the Gelugpa, together with important Tibetan officials, went to Mongolia to receive the child who had been recognised as the true reincarnation of the Third Dalai Lama by no less a figure than the abbot of Gaden monastery. During the recognition ceremony he was able to say the names of all the attendants of the earlier incarnation, including the Nepalese sculptor who had made the principal Buddha image for Lithang monastery which the previous incarnation had founded. The boy was given the name of

Yonten Gyatso. His parents, however, refused to part with their son until he was older. Consequently Yonten Gyatso was given religious education in Mongolia by Tibetan lamas. When he was twelve years old, the Tibetan lamas insisted that he be taken to Tibet.

Yonten Gyatso was escorted to Tibet accompanied by his father, Tibetan officials and lamas and a thousand Mongol cavalrymen.

In *Tibet: A Political History,* the late Tsepon W.D. Shakabpa, a noted Tibetan historian and diplomat, wrote: 'When

Yonten Gyatso arrived at Lhasa, he was given official recognition at a ceremony arranged by the monastic officials and was enthroned as the Fourth Dalai Lama. He was initiated into monkhood by the ex-Gaden Tripa (the chief abbot of Gaden monastery, the highest ordained monk in the Gelug hierarchy and the principal lineage-holder of Tsongkapa's order), Sangay Rinchen. While a student-monk at Drepung monastery, he was visited by the humble, but scholarly lama from Tashilhunpo, Lobsang Chogyen, under whom he continued his studies.'

Lobsang Chogyen posthumously became the First Panchen Lama, the principal incarnate lama of Tashilhunpo monastery and the second highest Gelug spiritual leader of the Tibetan people.

Yonten Gyatso later became the abbot of Drepung and then Sera. In 1616, at the age of twenty-eight, he died at Drepung monastery.

## NGAWANG LOBSANG GYATSO
### The Fifth Dalai Lama

The Fifth Dalai Lama was born in 1617 in Chongye, south of Lhasa—the cradle of Tibetan civilisation. When Sonam Choephel, the chief attendant of the Fourth Dalai Lama heard of the exceptional abilities of the Chongye boy, he paid a visit to the child and showed him articles belonging to the previous Dalai Lama. The child at once said that those belonged to him. Sonam Choephel kept the discovery of the Fifth Dalai Lama a secret because of the turbulent political situation. When things settled down, the Fifth Dalai Lama was taken to Drepung monastery where he was ordained into monkhood by Lobsang Chogyen, the future Panchen Lama.

The Fifth Dalai Lama was recognised at a time when Tibet was in political turmoil. However, all this uncertainty was laid to rest by Gushri Khan, the chief of the Qoshot Mongols, who sided with the Gelug church in its struggle with the Kagyu sect. In 1642 the Dalai Lama was led in state to Shigatse, power base of the Kagyu, the main rival of the Gelug church, and was enthroned as both the spiritual and political leader of Tibet. On two lower thrones sat Gushri Khan and Sonam Choephel, the

population of western Tibet and in 1648 he had a census taken in eastern Tibet, the areas in Kham, and collected taxes from the landholders.

From 1649 to 1651, Sunzhi, the Manchu emperor, invited the Dalai Lama to Peking—a journey he set out on in 1652.

Desi or Regent. The Mongol chieftain offered the Fifth Dalai Lama *mendel tensum,* a symbolic offering of a gold image of the Buddha, a book and a small stupa, representing the body, speech and mind of the Buddha, respectively.

Despite minor revolts, the reign of the Fifth Dalai Lama was largely peaceful. In 1643 the Dalai Lama took a census of the

✿ *The Fourteenth Dalai Lama imparting his annual religious teachings in Dharamsala.* FACING PAGE: *Refugees and pilgrims hope the bell of religious freedom will ring in Tibet again.*

The Panchen Lama came from Tsang to Dam, some distance to the north of Lhasa and the whole party remained there for six days. Gushri Khan and Sonam Choephel accompanied the Dalai Lama for a day.

Throughout his journey, Tibetan and Mongol nomads came to receive his blessing. When the Dalai Lama reached the Chinese province of Ningxia, he was

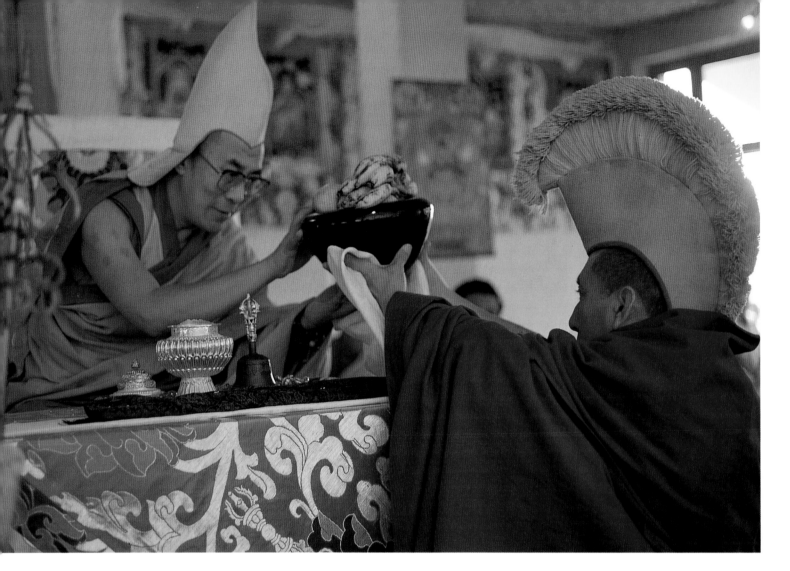

greeted by the emperor's minister and military commander who came with three thousand cavalry to escort the Tibetan leader. The emperor himself travelled from Peking and greeted the Tibetan leader at a place called Kothor. In the Chinese capital the Dalai Lama stayed at the Yellow Palace, built for him by the emperor, and on the first day of the first month of 1653, according to the Tibetan lunar calendar, all the officials of Peking came there to pay respects to him. When the emperor officially met the Dalai Lama, the two of them exchanged titles. The same year, the Dalai Lama returned to Tibet.

Gushri Khan died in 1655 as did

☼ *'May you live for eternity to show the path to liberation to all the suffering sentient beings'—a long-life offering to the Dalai Lama.*

Sonam Choephel. The latter was succeeded to the post of *Desi* by Trinlay Gyatso. When the Emperor died in 1662, his son, K'ang-si, ascended the Manchu throne, and in the same year the Panchen Lama died at the age of ninety-one. In 1665 Tashilhunpo monastery petitioned the Dalai Lama, requesting him to recognise a three-year-old boy born in Topgyal in the Tsang region as the Second Panchen Lama. The Dalai Lama accepted the request and gave the boy the name of Lobsang Yeshi.

In 1675 the Dalai Lama asked for the resignation of Losang Thubtop, the *Desi*. The members of the Gelug school of Tibetan Buddhism are celibates. Yet the

*Desi*, who had taken the vows of a monk, kept a mistress and when the Dalai Lama heard this, he asked him to resign. He appointed Sangye Gyatso as the new *Desi*.

The Fifth Dalai Lama died in 1682 at the age of sixty-eight, while isolated in a three-year retreat. He was a man of few words, but what he said carried conviction and influenced rulers beyond the borders of Tibet. Although Gelugpa, he retained the services of several prominent lamas from other sects. Though Gelug lamas were critical of this, the Dalai Lama dismissed their objections and said that he preferred to be familiar with the beliefs and teachings of the rival schools rather than being ignorant of them. He was a great scholar, well versed in Sanskrit. He wrote many books, including one on poetry. He established two institutions, one for lay officials and another for monk officials, where they were taught Mongolian, Sanskrit, astrology, poetry, archery, horse riding and administration.

## TSANGYANG GYATSO
### The Sixth Dalai Lama

The Sixth Dalai Lama was a tragic figure. But he is one of the best loved of Tibet's Dalai Lamas. His love of wine and the company of women was shrugged off by a tolerant society and his songs and poems still remain on the lips of Tibetans today.

Tsangyang Gyatso was born on March 1, 1683, in the region of Mon in present-day Arunachal Pradesh. In order to complete

✿ *'May the darkness of my ignorance be dispelled by the light of your wisdom.'*

the Potala Palace, *Desi* Sangye Gyatso carried out the wishes of the Fifth Dalai Lama and kept his death a secret for fifteen years. People were told that the Great Fifth was continuing his long retreat. Meals were taken to his chamber and on important occasions the Dalai Lama's ceremonial gown was placed on the throne. However, when Mongol princes insisted on having an audience, an old monk called Depa Deyrab of Namgyal monastery, who resembled the Dalai Lama, was hired to pose in his place. He wore a hat and an eye shade to conceal the fact that he lacked the Dalai Lama's piercing eyes. The *Desi* managed to maintain this charade till he heard that a boy in Mon exhibited remarkable abilities. He sent his trusted attendants to the area and, in 1688, the boy was brought to Nankartse, a place near Lhasa. There he was educated by teachers appointed by the *Desi* until 1697, when the *Desi* sent his trusted minister, Shabdrung Ngawang Shonu to the Manchu court to inform Emperor K'ang-si of the death of the Fifth and the discovery of the Sixth Dalai Lama. He announced the fact to the people of Tibet, who greeted the news with gratitude and joy and thanked the *Desi* for saving them from lamenting the setting of the sun and instead, making them rejoice in its rising.

The *Desi* invited the Second Panchen Lama to Nankartse where Tibet's second highest religious leader administered the *getsul* vows—the vows of a novice monk—to the youth and named him Tsangyang Gyatso. In October 1697, the fourteen-year-old was enthroned as the Sixth Dalai Lama in a ceremony attended by Tibetan government officials, representatives of the three major monasteries—Sera, Gaden and Drepung—Mongol princes, representatives of Emperor K'ang-si and the Lhasa populace.

With the enthronement ceremony over, a long period of strict religious training awaited the Dalai Lama. The *Desi* himself taught the Dalai Lama religious and political matters and requested the Panchen Lama and other high lamas to

✿ *The temple in Bodh Gaya, which towers over the Bodhi tree under which the Buddha attained enlightenment. FACING PAGE: The statue of the Shakyamuni Buddha in Jokhang, Lhasa, is the holiest image in Tibet. It is said to have been sculpted in India during the lifetime of the Buddha.*

give spiritual instruction to groom the young Dalai Lama to rule.

But this was not to be. Tsangyang Gyatso had other ideas. He loved the outdoor life, and had no plans to take the *gelong* vows, the pledges of a fully-ordained monk. In fact, he visited the Panchen Lama in Shigatse and after prostrating three times and requesting his forgiveness, renounced even the vows of a novice monk. He dressed as a layman, preferring robes of light blue silk and brocade; kept his hair long and wore conspicuous rings on several fingers. Though he continued to live in the Potala Palace, he roamed in Lhasa and other outlying villages, spending his days with his friends in the park behind the Potala Palace practising archery, and nights in taverns in Lhasa and Shol (an area below the Potala) drinking *chang,* singing love songs and meeting his numerous lovers. The doors of those taverns in Lhasa and Shigatse which were frequented by Tsangyang Gyatso were, thereafter, always painted yellow as a consecration of the highest honour.

But this lifestyle impacted tragically on the politics of Tibet. Lhasang Khan, the descendant of Gushri Khan and the nominal king of Tibet, was disgusted by the Dalai Lama's behaviour and blamed *Desi* Sangye Gyatso. He also refused to remain just a figurehead and wanted to assert himself in the affairs of Tibet. *Desi* Sangye Gyatso then made a mistake. He

✿ *The Dalai Lama and his Gelug school placed great importance on debating. PAGES 96-97: The Potala Palace as viewed from Chakpori Hill on which was located Tibet's old medical college.*

turned to Galdan, the chief of the Dzungar Mongols who dominated the Ili Valley in present-day Xinjiang or eastern Turkestan. The Dzungars were rivals of the Qoshot Mongol tribes and were viewed with increasing nervousness by Emperor K'ang-si because of their rapid expansion along the borders of China.

With the Manchu court behind him, Lhasang Khan invaded Tibet, killed Sangye Gyatso and took Tsangyang Gyatso to the Kokonor region where he met his death in 1706 in mysterious circumstances.

Though Tsangyang Gyatso's reign was a tragic failure, he is well remembered for his love songs:

I dwell apart in Potala;
A god on earth am I;
But in town the prince of rogues
And boisterous revelry.
Lo! the Serpent Gods and demons
Lurk behind me stern and mighty;
Sweet the apple grows before me;
Fear leads nowhere; I must pluck it.
Dear love, to whom my heart goes out,
If only we could wed,
Then I would have gained the choicest gem
From the ocean's deepest bed.
Last year the crop was young and green
Tis now but withered strands;
And youth grown old is dried and bent
Like bows from southern lands.

In this life's short walk
We have had our share of joy.
Let us hope to meet again
In the youth of our next life.

## KELSANG GYATSO
### The Seventh Dalai Lama

In retrospect, the Tibetans believed that Tsangyang Gyatso predicted his own rebirth at Lithang in Kham when he wrote this song:

White crane, lend me your wings,
I go no farther than Lithang,
And thence, return again.

Sure enough, the Seventh Dalai Lama was born in 1708, two years after the disappearance of the Sixth. The monks of Thubten Jampaling monastery, which was founded in Lithang by the Third Dalai Lama, were astonished by the wonders of the child. Soon news of the birth of the Lithang child reached the ears of Lhasang Khan who had imposed a new Dalai Lama on Tibet, alleged to be his son. But after much political intrigue and fighting, (see Chapter 2), Kelsang Gyatso was enthroned as the Seventh Dalai Lama in 1720. Lhasang Khan's Dalai Lama was deposed and sent to China. When the Seventh Dalai Lama's recognition was confirmed, Emperor Kangxi wrote a letter to Tibet's new ruler: 'I was made very happy on the day the Dalai Lama was confirmed. He is a true reincarnation. The Dalai Lama is a like a ray of sunshine, which is impossible for any one group of people to obscure. The ray of Buddhist faith will shine on everyone through him. The Mongols in the Kokonor region should remain united and friendly instead of quarrelling among themselves. The Dalai Lama is requested to advise them to remain obedient to the emperor.'

The Seventh Dalai Lama abolished the post of *Desi* as it placed too much power in one man's hands, and, instead, constituted the *kashag* or council of ministers to administer the country. Otherwise, the Seventh Dalai Lama refrained from participating in the affairs of Tibet, letting his ministers handle all matters. He devoted himself to religious matters. The Seventh Dalai Lama was a scholar and wrote many books, specially on the *tantras*. He was also a great poet who, unlike Tsangyang Gyatso, dwelt on spiritual themes. His simple and unblemished life won him the hearts of all Tibetans. He died in 1757.

## JAMPEL GYATSO
### The Eighth Dalai Lama

Jampel Gyatso was born in 1758 at Lhari Gang in the Tsang region of south-western Tibet. His father, Sonam Dhargye, and mother, Phuntsok Wangmo, were originally from Kham and traced their ancestry to Dhrala Tsegyal, one of the legendary heroes of the Gesar epic.

As soon as Jampel Gyatso was

☼ *FACING PAGE: The last photograph of the Great Thirteenth Dalai Lama.*

conceived, Lhari Gang was blessed with a bumper harvest with each stalk of barley bearing three, four or five ears—something unprecedented. When the mother and a relative were having their supper in the garden, a huge rainbow appeared, one end of which touched the mother's shoulder. (This is considered to be a very auspicious portent, associated with the birth of a holy being).

Just before the birth of Jampel Gyatso, the local women were celebrating their folk dance festival, when, by some miraculous inspiration, one woman burst into the following refrain:

On the ridge of Lhari Gang

A lotus flower was born;

The lotus opened its petals

And filled the world with its brilliance.

A spontaneous refrain from another woman went like this:

Kushok (Dalai Lama) came to Tsang,

Tsang's barley became more nutritious.

The sun rose from Tsang

And radiated to Central Tibet.

This is not the sun's radiance;

This is the Dalai Lama's radiance.

The Dalai Lama's huge radiance

Illuminated the Potala Palace.

Not long after his birth, Jampel Gyatso was frequently observed to be looking heavenward with a smile on his face. He was also seen to be attempting to sit in a meditative, lotus posture. When Palden Yeshi, the Third Panchen Lama, heard about this boy, he pronounced: 'This is the authentic reincarnation of the Dalai Lama.' Tibet's primary protector, entered the body of a village doctor and prophesied: 'To Lhari Gang has come the authentic reincarnation of the Meaningful to Behold, the Gem of the Sky. I, Dorje Drakden, have come into this body to serve him in the four seasons.'

As the child began to speak, he said: 'I will go to Lhasa at the age of three.' Now the whole of Tibet was convinced that this child was the Eighth Dalai Lama. Drakpa Thaye, the chief attendant of the Seventh Dalai Lama, came to Lhasa with a large contingent of lamas and Tibetan government officials. They took the boy, then two-and-a-half years old, to Tashilhunpo monastery in Shigatse, and performed the recognition ceremony. All the dignitaries at the ceremony were struck by the similarity in the personalities of the young boy and his predecessor.

After the ceremony, the child was escorted to Lhasa and enthroned in the Potala. The enthronement ceremony was presided over by Demo Tulku Jampel Yeshi, who was the first Regent to represent the Dalai Lamas when they were minors. In addition to his remarkable spiritual legacy, it was the Eight Dalai Lama who, in 1783, built the fabled Norbulingka Park and Summer Palace on the outskirts of Lhasa. The Eight Dalai Lama died in 1804.

### The Ninth, Tenth, Eleventh and Twelfth Dalai Lamas

Each of these four Dalai Lamas died very young. The Ninth, Lungtok Gyatso, was born in 1805 and died in the spring of 1815. The Tenth Dalai Lama lived the longest. Tsultrim Gyatso was born in 1816 and was recognised and enthroned in 1822, but he was constantly in poor health and died in 1837 at the age of twenty-one. The Eleventh Dalai Lama, Khedrub Gyatso, born in Gathar in Kham, was enthroned in 1855 and died within a year and the Twelfth, Trinley Gyatso, was born in 1856 and died at the age of nineteen.

### THUBTEN GYATSO
### The Thirteenth Dalai Lama

The recognition of Thubten Gyatso as the Thirteenth Dalai Lama was greeted by an ecstactic British Viceroy with these words which are tinged with a degree of sarcasm directed towards a uniquely Asian method of coming up with leaders: 'We were plunged in sorrow at the news of your untimely passing away but your speedy rebirth filled us with happiness.'

The early life of the Thirteenth Dalai Lama was anything but happy. He was born in 1876 into a peasant family in Dagpo in south Tibet. He was recognised as the reincarnation of the Dalai Lama in 1878 and enthroned a year later. He survived an assassination attempt and had to constantly grapple with the legacy of his four predecessors having died young. He

☼ *The Thirteenth Dalai Lama was able to re-assert the power of his institution.*

assumed political power in 1895 before he became 19 years old and was thrown thick into the Great Game played out by Czarist Russia and British India on the fringes of their sprawling empires. As recounted in detail in Chapter 3, he went through the British invasion of Tibet in 1904 and the Chinese invasion of his country in 1909 and survived both experiences, with his authority enormously enhanced.

When the news spread in 1909 that Chao Er-feng, the Chinese General, was at the gates of Lhasa, the Dalai Lama and some of the most important officials fled Lhasa and headed to India. The group crossed Dromo and negotiated the Jelep-la pass which separates Tibet from Sikkim and halted the night at Gnatong in a cluster of log huts which served as the telegraph office linking Tibet with India. Sergeants Luff and Humphreys manned the office. In the middle of the night they heard hammering at the office door.

'Who's there?'

No reply.

Again there was knocking and the two soldiers opened the door and found a gathering of the most excited Tibetans the two of them had ever come across.

'Who the hell are you?' asked Luff.

The answer came: 'The Dalai Lama.'

Luff asked, 'Which of you blighters is the Dalai Lama?'

The crowd said, 'He's coming.'

Luff shot back, 'Then who the hell told you to come here? Take your Dalai Lama to the regular dak bungalow. It's much more comfortable.'

Soon after the Dalai Lama showed up, and one Tibetan said, 'Here's the Dalai Lama.'

Luff wasn't done as yet. He said, 'Now which blighter is the correct Dalai Lama. All of you seem to think you are the Dalai Lama.'

Then the crowd explained to Luff and Humphreys how the Dalai Lama and his party were being pursued by Chinese soldiers.

Even if Luff might not have been convinced of the authenticity of the correct Dalai Lama, the Thirteenth managed to do this to some of his monk retainers years later in the most authoritative way.

In 1911, the Manchu Dynasty was overthrown and the Tibetans took the opportunity of expelling the remnant Manchu forces from Tibet. The Dalai Lama returned to Tibet and went on to exercise political authority not seen since the reign of the Fifth Dalai Lama. Besides attempting to modernise Tibet, the Dalai Lama also tried to eliminate some of the more oppressive features of the Tibetan monastic system. One touched on the Monlam Chenmo or the Great Prayer Festival which was established by Tsongkapa. The Fifth Dalai Lama had introduced the system of handing over the administration of the city of Lhasa to two monk judges for the period of twenty-one days during the Great Prayer Festival. This, he said, was a symbol that in Tibet,

✿ *In his life the Thirteenth Dalai Lama went into exile to Mongolia, China and India.*
*FACING PAGE: The Great Thirteenth Dalai Lama.*
*Pages 106-107: His Holiness welcomes Losar, the Tibetan New Year, on the roof of the main temple in Dharamsala.*

religion was the ultimate authority. However, this resulted in many abuses and heavy fines were imposed on trifling matters and the people of Lhasa escaped the city to avoid excessive taxation by the two monk judges. The Thirteenth Dalai Lama decided to put a stop to this form of corruption but the two monk judges refused to comply. He sent for them and asked, 'By whose authority do you exercise this power?'

'By the authority of the Great Fifth Dalai Lama,' they replied.

'And who is the Great Fifth Dalai Lama?' the young ruler asked.

Greatly surprised, the two replied, 'Without doubt, Your Holiness is he.'

Since that confrontation the Dalai Lama succeeded in stamping out the worst abuses of the Great Prayer Festival and the grateful people of Lhasa stopped fleeing the city during the festival.

While in exile the Dalai Lama was fascinated with the inventions of the modern world. He was particularly impressed with the telephone. Writes Sir Charles Bell, the British political officer for Sikkim, Bhutan and Tibet, in *Portrait of a Dalai Lama:* 'I was in an annexe close to Hastings House, and a private telephone connected the two buildings. The Precious Protector liked talking on this. He enjoyed it so much that the conversation used to terminate in a gurgle of laughter from his end.'

# Tenzin Gyatso: The Fourteenth
# DALAI LAMA

In the year of the Water Bird, 1933, the Great Thirteenth Dalai Lama passed away. Two years later Reting Rinpoche, the Regent, and the Tibetan government took the first steps in the complicated and onerous search for the next Dalai Lama.

According to age-old spiritual tradition, the Regent and the Tibetan government consulted oracles and lamas for signs and clues of where the next Dalai Lama would be born. Strange cloud formations were seen to the north-east of Lhasa. The body of the Thirteenth Dalai

*✿ FACING PAGE: His Holiness the Fourteenth Dalai Lama*

Lama, placed on a throne in the Norbulingka palace, had been facing south. Soon astonished attendants recalled that the body was facing in the direction of the north-east. But the conclusive divine indication that the next Dalai Lama would be born in north-east Tibet came from the sacred lake Lhami Latso which the Regent consulted in 1935.

Search parties combed Tibet, looking for that special boy who would hold the destiny of the Tibetan people. Finally the Dalai Lama was discovered in Amdo in the person of a two-year-old boy called Lhamo

Dhondup. He was four when he made the long journey to Lhasa in 1939. This is how the Fourteenth Dalai Lama describes his entry into the city: 'By now our party was very large, and we marched on in a long procession towards the Holy City. On both sides of our route thousands of monks lined up in rows with coloured banners... The whole population of Lhasa—men and women, young and old—thronged together in their best clothes to receive and welcome me with homage. As they watched me passing, I could hear them crying, "The day of our happiness has come..."'

Lhamo Dhondup, born on July 6, 1935, was enthroned in 1940 at the age of

*His Holiness the Dalai Lama, accompanied by Khamba guerrillas, on his way to India.*

five as the new Dalai Lama. So began the education of the Dalai Lama, who divided his time between the Potala and the Norbulingka. The Dalai Lama considered the Potala too confining and preferred the poplar-lined spacious open parks around his summer palace. In a recent interview, the Dalai Lama said: 'I always enjoyed leaving the Potala and going to the summer palace, Norbulingka, at the official start of summer. The season was most beautiful, all the lawns were turning green, the apricot trees flowering and the birds singing.'

Whether in the Potala or Norbulingka, he spent his boyhood in the company of grown-up men, concentrating on his

spiritual education, but now and then he pursued his own interests. One of these involved playing with mechanical toys and wristwatches. In his autobiography, *My Land and My People*, the Dalai Lama says: 'When I was small, kind people who knew of this interest sometimes sent me mechanical toys, such as cars and boats and airplanes. But I was never content to play with them for long—I always had to take them to pieces to see how they worked. Usually I managed to put them together again, though sometimes, as might be expected, there were disasters ... Later on, I was given an old movie projector which was operated by turning a

⚙ *'Strange are the ways*
*of destiny*
*which sometimes gives*
*oblique hints*
*of things to come;*
*though undeciphered*
*the hints remain;*
*as a little kid*
*the Takser lad*
*would often of his dresses*
*a bundle make*
*and playing the pilgrim*
*announce:*
*"To Lhasa, to Lhasa*
*I go!"'*

Prof. Parmananda Sharma
Chenresi: The Story of the
Fourteenth Dalai Lama

handle, and when I took that to pieces, I found batteries which worked its electric light. That was my first introduction to electricity, and I puzzled over the connections all alone until I found the way to make it go. I had success (though this was later) with my wristwatch. I took that entirely to pieces to study its principles and it still worked when I put it together again ... One of the minor pleasures of the Norbulingka was that it had a motor generator for electric light, which often broke down, so that I had every excuse to take it to pieces. From that machine, I discovered how internal combustion engines work, and also noticed how the

dynamo created a magnetic field when it turned—and I must say that I managed to mend it more often than not.'

*✿ The Fourteenth Dalai Lama was recognised at the age of two and enthroned as the Dalai Lama in 1940.*

One of the memorable periods of the young Dalai Lama was when he managed to turn a rusting Dodge and an Austin siren into up-and-running condition. The Thirteenth Dalai Lama had been presented with two 1927 Baby Austins and a 1931 orange Dodge, first carried in pieces over the Himalayas and then reassembled in Lhasa because there was no motorable road linking Tibet with India. Since the death of the Great Thirteenth, these cars had been abandoned to gather dust and rust. With the help of a young Indian-trained Tibetan driver, the Dalai Lama put the Dodge back in working order. He did the same with an Austin by borrowing parts from the other. Probably this was the first time in Tibetan history that two cars were repaired in Lhasa and the Dalai Lama described those days as exciting moments. Even today the Dalai Lama sometimes spends his rare moments of leisure repairing damaged wristwatches of acquaintances in a workshop at his residence in Dharamsala. The Dalai Lama says that very often he's able to return the wristwatches intact and functioning to their astonished but grateful owners.

However, the joys of childhood were soon over for the young Dalai Lama; Tibet's precarious status and international politics put an end to his boyhood happiness.

In 1950, when communist China was banging at the door of Tibet, a nervous Tibetan government requested the young Dalai Lama to assume full political responsibility of the country. The Dalai Lama remembers: 'This filled me with

anxiety. I was only sixteen. (Tibetans calculate a person's age from the time of conception and not from the birth date: hence, His Holiness adds a year to his age.) I was far from having finished my religious education. I knew nothing about the world and had no experience of politics, and yet I was old enough to know how ignorant I was and how much I had still to learn... I saw that at such a serious moment in our history, I could not refuse my responsibilities. I had to shoulder them, put my boyhood behind me, and immediately prepare myself to lead my country, as well as I was able, against the vast power of Communist China.'

✿ *His Holiness the Dalai Lama and members of his family in India in 1956 when he came to attend the Buddha Jayanti commemoration.*

China forced a reluctant but utterly defeated Tibet to sign the 17-point treaty which promised that Tibet's traditional social structure, its religion and the powers and privileges of the Dalai Lama would be kept intact. In return for this guarantee, Tibet was forced to agree to become a part of China.

In 1954, the Dalai Lama made a trip to China to meet with all the top Chinese leaders, including Mao Tse-tung who told an astonished Dalai Lama that religion was poison—a statement which indicated the impending tragedy which Tibet would undergo. Buddhist Tibet's honeymoon with communist China did not last long. The

simmering Tibetan resentment exploded in the open in March 1959 when the Tibetans in Lhasa rose up to shake off the communist yoke. The uprising was easily and bloodily quashed and the Dalai Lama and members of his government fled to India.

So unfamiliar was Tibet in the mid-twentieth century that when the Dalai Lama arrived on Indian soil, the two hundred reporters gathered in Tezpur in Assam, went through a frustrating ritual of identifying the real Dalai Lama. This game was played out between the two news agency rivals, Associated Press and the United Press.

The United Press correspondent sent to his head office what he thought was the photograph of the Dalai Lama. He received a frantic cable back: 'Your Dalai Lama not Associated Press Dalai Lama stop Check.'

The United Press reporter responded: 'My Dalai Lama right Dalai Lama.'

The United Press head office replied: 'Your Dalai Lama has hair stop Check.'

The United Press correspondent had realised his mistake by this time and responded:

'Kill my Dalai Lama stop Mistake.'

Instead of the Dalai Lama, he had taken a photograph of the interpreter!

Despite this whimsical episode the story the foreign correspondents were covering was not a happy one. While the rest of the world was dismantling colonialism, these reporters were witness to the restructuring of a new kind of colonialism, though China's successful

☼ *Taktser village, birth place of the present Dalai Lama. Top: Mrs. Jetsun Pema, the younger sister of His Holiness with a photo of Gyalyum Chenmo, their mother.*

portrayal of Tibet's old political system as feudal gave this form of colonialism a ring of being a true liberation.

Colonialism or liberation—the victims were the Tibetan people, whose ranks were decimated by a series of violent campaigns which China conducted in Tibet. In all, China's mopping-up exercise in the aftermath of the 1959 uprising, plus the Great Leap Forward Famine and the Cultural Revolution which both engulfed Tibet, claimed the lives of approximately 1.2 million Tibetans out of a population of

*✿ Increasing attraction of Buddhism brings regular foreign students and visitors to Dharamsala.*

six million and resulted in the destruction of more than six thousand monasteries, temples and other institutions of learning.

While this was going on in Tibet, in India the Dalai Lama set up his Government-in-exile and successfully nurtured a cohesive Tibetan refugee community. He democratised his administration by promulgating Tibet's first written constitution and set up the Tibetan parliament with its members elected by the refugees. With the assistance of the Indian government, he created a modern Tibetan school system. It was only after he managed to build a viable and vibrant Tibetan refugee community that he launched into a sustained international campaign to garner support for the cause of Tibet. His efforts resulted in the creation of an enormous and still-growing international constituency to restore Tibet's rights.

After the death of Mao Tse-tung in 1976, China entered a period of liberalisation. Chinese leaders invited the Dalai Lama to send representatives to Tibet to assess the situation there. The Dalai Lama sent four fact-finding missions

to Tibet and two exploratory delegations to tackle the real business of negotiating with the Chinese government.

In 1987 the Dalai Lama addressed the United States' Congress in Washington D.C., unveiling his Five-Point Peace Plan for Tibet which called on China to transform Tibet into a zone of peace, respect the fundamental human rights of the Tibetan people, halt its population transfer into Tibet, respect the environmental and ecological integrity of the Tibetan plateau and negotiate on the issue of Tibet.

✿ *Public audience in Dharamsala: people from all parts of the world eager to meet His Holiness the Dalai Lama.*

In 1988, at a sitting of the European Parliament in Strasbourg, France, the Dalai Lama outlined his Strasbourg Proposal in which he conceded that Tibet would be willing to become a self-governing, democratic political entity in association with the People's Republic of China.

Both these proposals were rejected by China as being a disguised form of Tibetan independence. In exile, the response was outrage from the younger refugees who considered the second proposal a sell-out.

Meanwhile, in 1989 China went through the Tiananmen Square massacre

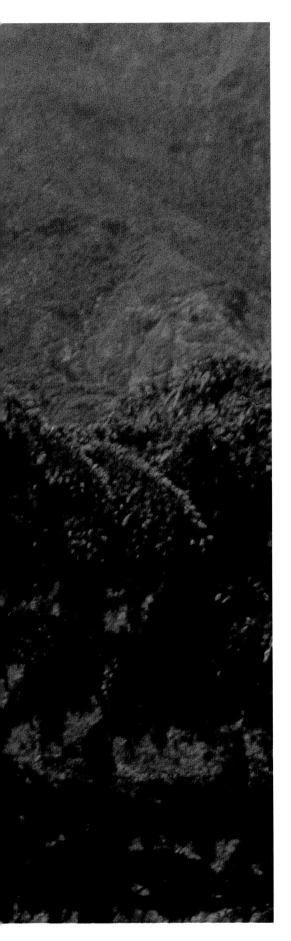

☼ *ABOVE: His Holiness and behind him is Sakya Trizin (with hair), the head of the Sakya school of Tibetan Buddhism. LEFT: His Holiness the Dalai Lama seen with the all-important umbrella in Dharamsala—a place which receives the second highest rainfall during the monsoons in India.*

when hundreds, if not thousands, of Chinese students were killed simply because they demanded democracy and more accountability of the government to the Chinese people. That year the international community gave belated recognition to the efforts of the Dalai Lama by awarding him the Nobel Peace Prize. He was honoured with the prize for his constructive and forward-looking proposals for the solution of international conflicts, human rights issues, and global environmental problems. But mainly he

was awarded the prize for his consistent opposition to the use of violence in his struggle for the liberation of Tibet.

Reacting to his being awarded the Nobel Peace Prize, the Dalai Lama said that it did not add to or subtract from his true vocation of being a Buddhist monk. But he said in his acceptance speech that he was happy to receive it on behalf of the six million Tibetans because this award represents worldwide recognition and

support for the just cause of the Tibetan people's struggle for freedom and self-determination.

Many are curious about the personality of the present Dalai Lama. This is best brought out by Robert Kiely who writes in *The Good Heart*, 'It has been said that the Dalai Lama is a simple man. Though this may be meant as a compliment, it is difficult to associate such a label from a Western tendency to condescend to the

✿ *ABOVE: His Holiness leads a peace march.*
*FACING PAGE (TOP): With Nelson Mandela in South Africa in 1997.*
*FACING PAGE (BELOW): December 1989: The Dalai Lama receiving the Nobel Peace Prize in Stockholm.*

religions and cultures of the East, treating them as exotic but philosophically primitive traditions. Insofar as he is earthy, direct, warm and *simpatico*, the Dalai Lama may be called "simple"; but in every other sense, he is subtle, quick, complex, and an extraordinarily intelligent and learned man. He brings three qualities to a spiritual discourse—traits so rare in some contemporary Christian circles as to have elicited gasps of relieved gratitude from the audience—qualities of gentleness, clarity, and laughter…

'His reading of the meeting between Mary Magdalene and Jesus in St. Johns account of the Resurrection brought many to tears. It would be hard to say why. Some said later that it was as if they were hearing the words for the first time, as though their tenderness and mystery and beauty had been taken for granted and were brought to life again, like a gift from an unexpected courier.'

In recent years, Hollywood released two films based on the life of the young Dalai Lama: *Seven Years in Tibet* and *Kundun,* which won several Oscars. In an interview the Dalai Lama was asked what he thought about this tinsel-world fuss being made over him. He said: 'Personally, I do not have much feeling. But regarding more awareness about Tibet—then these films are certainly very useful.'

Here are some more snapshots of the Dalai Lama, the man and his beliefs. Constantly asked to define his religion, the Dalai Lama says, 'My religion is kindness.'

Asked to describe himself, the Dalai Lama says: 'I'm a simple Buddhist monk.'

Asked what gives him the greatest source of inspiration, the Dalai Lama quotes this stanza from Shantideva, an

✿ *A novice monk recites his daily prayers.*
*FACING PAGE: His Holiness the Dalai Lama won the Nobel Peace Prize in 1989 for his constructive peace initiatives.*

Indian Buddhist mystic:

As long as space endures,
As long as suffering remains,
May I too abide
To dispel the misery of the world.

*Tibet: Land of Snows* by Giuseppe Tucci, Oxford & IBH Publishing Co., 1967

*The Water-Horse and Other Years: A History of 17th and 18th Century Tibet* by K. Dhondup, Library of Tibetan Works and Archives, 1984

*My Land and My People* by the Dalai Lama, McGraw-Hill Book Company, Inc., 1962

*The Status of Tibet: History, Rights, and Prospects in International Law* by Michael C. Walt van Praag, Westview, 1987

*The Search for Modern China* by Jonathan D. Spence, W.W. Norton & Company, 1990

*Portrait of a Dalai Lama: Life and Times of the Great Thirteenth* by Sir Charles Bell, William Collins, 1946

*A Cultural History of Tibet* by David Snellgrove and Hugh Richardson, George Weidenfeld and Nicholson Ltd., 1968

*The Government and Politics of Tibet* by Ram Rahul, Vikas Publications, 1969

*Tibet: A Political History* by Tsepon W.D. Shakabpa, Yale University Press, 1967

*The Necklace of Gem,* compiled and published by the office of His Holiness the Dalai Lama, Dharamsala, 1977

*Tibet: 25 Years of Struggle and Reconstruction,* Department of Information and International Relations, Central Tibetan Administration, 1984

*A History of Modern Tibet, 1913-1951* by Melvyn C. Goldstein, University of California Press, 1989

*How the Swans Came to the Lake: A Narrative History of Buddhism in America* by Rick Fields, Shambala Publications, 1981

Tibetan Bulletin, January-February 1998, DIIR, CTA, Dharamsala

*Tibet In Revolt* by George Patterson, Faber and Faber, 1960

*A Brief History of Tibet,* published by the Department of Information and International Relations, Dharamsala, 1987

*The Snow Lion and the Dragon: China, Tibet, and the Dalai Lama* by Melvyn C. Goldstein, University of California Press, 1997

*The Good Heart: A Buddhist Perspective on the Teachings of Jesus,* Wisdom Publications, 1996

✿ *PAGES 124-125: Moments of intense contemplation—devotees gather to light lamps and pray to the Enlightened Ones for relief and peace.*

# PHOTO CREDITS